THE AGILE EXECUTIVE

THE AGILE EXECUTIVE

Embracing Career Risks and Rewards

MARIANNE BROADBENT

M
MELBOURNE BOOKS

Published by Melbourne Books
Level 9, 100 Collins Street,
Melbourne, VIC 3000
Australia
www.melbournebooks.com.au
info@melbournebooks.com.au

Title: The Agile Executive: Embracing Career
Risks and Rewards
Author: Marianne Broadbent
ISBN: 9781925556476

A catalogue record for this
book is available from the
National Library of Australia

www.arbiterLT.com/TheAgileExecutive

To Robert for encouraging and enabling the journey,
and to our children David, Andrew, Patrick and Katie for embracing it.

CONTENTS

INTRODUCTION

Being an agile executive is about understanding your strengths, leading with purpose, and making choices that are right for you and your situation. It's about understanding the trade-offs that each of us makes, being comfortable with that and getting on with our contribution—in whatever we do. It's about continuing to grow and evolve, no matter what stage of career or life we are in.

Over the past twelve years I have been a leadership advisor, working with many executives and managers to help them build and sustain the people part of their businesses. My work as a partner and co-owner of NGS Global has two parts to it: the first is about partnering with clients on executive search and recruitment (commonly known as headhunting), the second is about enabling teams and individuals regarding their strengths and career aspirations, while concurrently being, what one of our clients referred to as, a 'carefully blunt' sounding board.

A few years ago, I was getting requests to give many talks or workshops about combining my professional and personal life. This included more general things like how do you do what you do? How do you manage making difficult career decisions? How do you manage trade-offs and career risks? Early on I found these challenging, being much more comfortable on the professional side rather than talking about my personal journey. After all, I expect not many people would want to make some of the choices I made, and there is nothing necessarily better or worse about that. But, I was able to blend aspects of that journey with the perspective and context that I have now, and frame that in a way that seemed to provide a useful lens for others.

Then my daughter Katie shaped the challenge for this book by giving me an empty folio for Mother's Day. On the front cover was 'In My Mother's Words' and the rest was blank. She explained to me that it was about time I gathered some thoughts together about my 'blended life' and eclectic career and put them into some sort of order.

My objective is to provide insights on what makes for executive and management success—drawing on both the professional and the personal. Some of these insights tend to be more critical for women, who, from my experience, second-guess themselves far too much. It is about having a good sense of purpose, knowing your strengths, where you might need some support, making considered decisions and then leading yourself and others with resolve. We all have highs and lows, and none of us are perfect.

This book is also about how to be a 'guilt-free' executive and, particularly, how to be a 'guilt-free' female executive. Female managers and executives tend to have to make more choices more often and, to a greater extent than men, we are expected to justify or explain them. Over about five different careers, and all the travel that went with it, I was often asked how my husband managed with our four growing children when I was away. My standard response was, 'Well about as well as I manage when he is away'. I don't think he was ever asked that question. When we make considered choices, for my husband and I, it was just figuring out how to do the things that were important to us—blending work, family and friends. I came to realise that I did not do the 'guilt thing' and maybe that was a very positive approach.

The decisions we need to make aren't easy and we need to weigh up the trade-offs (as there are always trade-offs), but then get on with it. Those of us with real choices are the lucky ones, I count myself amongst those, but then sometimes we do also have to work at making our 'luck'.

An Eclectic Career Journey

My career has been a little unusual, particularly for someone who started her professional career in 1970. The career start was not unusual—as a high school teacher in Sydney's outer suburbs—but then it progressed to encompass about five different careers, alongside the parenting one.

Following eight or nine years of high school teaching, I transitioned into a Head Office consulting role. Then, after moving to Melbourne, I had a career shift with about eight months of freelance work before landing a role as a lecturer in what was then the library and information services department at RMIT University. Over another six years and some promotions, this transitioned to a Head of Department role in Information Services leading a considerable amount of change.

Alongside this and parenting four school age children I was completing a PhD part-time at Melbourne Business School (MBS) in an area that became a passion—the link between business and technology strategies and their implementation in large companies.

As I was completing my PhD, MBS offered me a position as Director of the Centre for Technology Management. My colleague Peter Weill and I completed a major international industry-funded program and published a book with Harvard Business School Press.

Then came the invitation to join the large US-headquartered advisory services firm Gartner. Leading businesses locally, regionally, then being part of an innovative global team, was a huge learning exercise. The experience of career diversity was raised another notch.

After six years at Gartner there was a second Harvard Business School Press book going through production, and I thought I had achieved what I could at Gartner at the time. I had some career options and took the invitation to re-join Melbourne Business School, this time as Associate Dean.

Then after a year or so, Gartner came back to me with another challenging role—to lead new product development globally as part of a major transformation program. It was too good an opportunity to turn down and the then Dean at MBS was understanding—as was my generous spirited husband, Robert, who knew it meant that the Qantas Melbourne/Los Angeles/New York crew would again get to see a lot of me.

All the while my friend, Mark Lelliott, was suggesting that at some stage I should come and work with him and his colleagues. I was not sure what that really meant, as taking on a partner role in a leadership consultancy and executive search firm would be yet another career shift. But that is what I did when we could see that the Gartner transformation was well on track to double digit growth.

That leadership advisory firm is now NGS Global and that is where I have been Managing Partner and co-owner with colleagues since 2007. This is the longest I have been in any role. The reason is that every day is different and the work is always stimulating. It is a privilege to be an integral part of the journey of so many individuals and organisations.

Both my academic and commercial roles have always involved quite a lot of writing and presentations, but usually about research and professional areas of interest to clients. I have written regular columns about technology management and leadership over the years. This career journey has meant many lessons along the way and has, thus, been pivotal to this book and its evolution.

Journeys on the Home Front

While my professional journey progressed, our kids—David, Andrew, Patrick, Katherine (Katie)— grew up, met and married partners, and had their own kids. Each has made their own journey and today we are lucky that they are not just our kids but also valued friends of ours, as are their partners.

Their journeys have meandered a bit too. From an initial interest in law to history and education (David), teaching to theatre and performance (Andrew), a determined jazz trumpeter who plays many genres and leads others in music (Patrick), and combining occupational therapy and student well-being (Katie).

Even my husband Robert veered from his PhD in chemistry to being CEO for industry, professional associations and regulatory bodies, none of which required a chemistry qualification.

The lesson for all of us is to study what you are passionate about as it is likely that you will succeed in that area—or it might be a great base for something else entirely. You never know where it might take you.

This book is about finding your passion and your purpose, focusing on what you are good at, and making considered decisions about risks and rewards. It will introduce you to the passions of others and how they shaped those into careers with meaning—careers that appear to have meandered but where the professional passion evolved along with the individual's personal journey.

We are each people with many different facets to our lives, or many 'faces', but how do we integrate those so that we thrive with the decisions that we make? Knowing ourselves well is important to being able to lead others well. We need to be able to build trust, through sharing some of our vulnerabilities, so that others will then trust us. It helps if we are continuous learners, with a good level of curiosity, who are able to glean insights from others.

The Agile Executive is in three parts: The first part of the book is about how we grow our careers through a series of decisions, rather than a pre-determined plan. The second part of the book is about how we lead others through change, and draws more on the professional work we do. We each have much to learn from others and the third part of the book brings together the learnings and insights from over twenty female executives and managers.

PART 1

LEAD YOURSELF WITH PURPOSE

The first part of the book is about how we grow our careers through a series of decisions, rather than a pre-determined plan. It draws on many of my own experiences, along with those of others with whom I have worked. We each have our comfort zones and inflection points, and we each seek different types of risks and rewards. We have to understand our strengths, use them well, and build our resilience along the way. There are always trade-offs and, having made a decision, we should not look back and feel guilty about what might have been. Sometimes, too, we engage in activities that reinforce our sense of guilt to others—we might not even realise it, but we need to stop doing it. We need to own our achievements and know our own story, and that particularly applies to women. We should know how to 'get noticed' in a good way, and glean a few tips from a search consultant.

1

RISKS, INFLECTIONS POINTS AND LEARNING

Career starting point are just that—starting points

There are no longer careers for life. There is not one set pathway to success. Professions that might once have offered structured progression, like law or accounting, are under threat. Teachers and tertiary sector educators are dealing with different student expectations and the potential commodification of some parts of their knowledge base. Much repetitive work is being, and will be, replaced by automation and artificial intelligence.

At the same time, we have great opportunities to use technology developments creatively. In the performance area, whole sets of new capabilities are being employed. In the health sector, many of us are benefitting from terrific developments, as we combine discoveries and new ways of doing things by linking the human and technology sides of health care.

It is this innovative thinking that is the key to success. Your career is now driven by your ability to understand your capabilities, your strengths, any important developmental needs, and what you really enjoy doing.

A friend of mine is a keen sailor. He always talks about having some kind of destination in mind, but the way you get there will vary according to the conditions.

It is not a straight path. You need to use the tiller to provide some direction. Sometimes you have to tack and put up different sails depending on the wind, the swell, and the obstacles along the way. And then you need to adjust and trim the sails as the wind changes direction and strengths.

Sometimes just travelling in a big circle around San Francisco Bay or Sydney Harbour is fine, if that is what you enjoy. Your career can be a bit like that. Careers grow through tacking, using the tiller, and sometimes trimming the sails—choices are made based on the circumstances at the time.

With the trajectory of change now around us, we should expect to have multiple careers throughout our working life. For those of us with opportunities, or who are able to make opportunities, continuing to grow and evolve might take us in quite different directions.

Take some examples: one of Disney's international technology executives started her career as a public relations consultant, a leading Ombudsman started her career as a pharmacist, one of Australia's Vice Chancellors was a research assistant in a commercial laboratory, a medical practitioner from rural India is now CEO of a large disability services organisation, a chemical engineer moved into banking and now uses her combined skills and experience to chair company boards, and a law and Asian languages graduate is a global health technology entrepreneur.

Each of these executives used their initial education and experience to build a varied and satisfying career, ending up in roles that they may never have seen themselves in, but their careers emerged from their passions, desires, self-knowledge and growth.

So, the first thing you need to ask yourself is: Where do you get real satisfaction and what type of growth do you want?

In questioning people about their careers, we often ask about their inflection points—what were the decisions you made, the big risks you took, or the career opportunity that really challenged you? Where did you take a career risk and how did it turn out?

Certainly, we won't always have the choices we want, or be able to choose between options. What will matter increasingly though is our ability and willingness to take risks—considered risks—to gain new or different capabilities and experiences that will give us some future options.

Once upon a time, I had a career plan. But my actual career took a very different path—or many different paths, in fact. It involved taking risks—most of which worked out, but some not as well as I might have wanted at the time.

This chapter will provide some insights into HOW I made many career decisions and what I saw as the risks at time.

These decisions are my key inflection points. They involved some use of the tiller, some tacking and some shifting of the sails.

The plan I had at the start of my career journey…

I am a bit of a planner and a list-maker. I had always planned to meet the right guy when I was about twenty-six, which was a 'mature' age to do that forty years ago. This would happen after I completed my university degree, qualified as a teacher, travelled the world and then established my career. Children might or might not happen at some stage. (Due to some minor medical issues, I was not convinced that I could have children, anyway.)

Well, that was not quite how it turned out. I met that guy when I was nineteen, became engaged just after my twentieth birthday, married before I was twenty-one, and got pregnant on our honeymoon. Another three children came along in the next eight years or so, some planned, some not so planned. (Fertility clearly was not my problem, and, if anything, I came to realise that I had the reverse issue.) We did agree to have four, although my husband has no recollection of this (he would have been happy with a few more). I was one of seven and he was the eldest of eight, so four seemed like a good compromise at the time.

When we married, Robert was in the early stages of his studies for a PhD in Chemistry, so of course he was still a student a few years later. This meant remaining in Australia till that was done and travel plans were on hold for a while. Then the two of us were about to become the three of us, so it was time to make some new plans.

I enrolled in some qualifying subjects for a Master of Arts degree with a particular emphasis on the sociology of organisations and anthropology. The plan was that I would return to work for the eight-week required post childbirth period to qualify for a maternity leave payment, which we needed to support ourselves. (This was the arcane system in place then—you qualified for your maternity leave pay once you had been back at work for over two months.) Then I would resign and return to full-time motherhood and part-time study.

The choices that were never made...

I started my secondary school teaching career in one of Sydney's toughest high schools suffering from lacklustre leadership. It was a newly established school where the principal and his deputy were both out of their depth in terms of dealing with its many challenges. But two years later I found myself on the staff of an inner Western Sydney girls' high school with great leadership.

So, when my eight weeks post-maternity leave was up, I found I was getting physically nauseous trying to resign. I went to see the Deputy Principal, Marie Lynch, for some advice.

Marie asked me what I really wanted to do the most: study, spend more time with our son David, or keep working full-time. The answer was I just did not know yet. She suggested I keep doing all three till I figured it out.

It was some of the best advice I have ever had—and she continued to ask me how things were going from time to time.

Three or four years later, my master's was completed, we'd had a second child, a third was on the way, and I was still working full-time—broken by short bouts of maternity leave. I'd never had to make that choice amongst the three options.

When Robert finally finished his PhD and got a paying job, we moved into our first home with a mortgage in the mid-1970s—a classic three-bedroom fibro with a sunroom added along the back. We had lived very frugally for many years to save the deposit we needed. We had to completely furnish the house as we had been renting furnished 'half-houses' till then, and the only pieces of furniture we owned were a piano and a roll top desk, which probably says something about what we valued at the time!

A sense of purpose and direction: more useful than a detailed plan

You have to work out what is best for you—and deal with situations as they arise.

My friend and former Gartner colleague, Robin Kranich, calls this the WHY, what is it that makes you want to leap out of bed and take on the world? Robin is Gartner's Executive Vice-President and Chief Human Relations Officer. Last summer, with two kids away at summer camp she took some time to reflect on what drives her, and her WHY in terms of the mark she wants to leave on the world. In her case, 'her world' is her family, friends and the 15,000 or so people she works with at Gartner. She wrote down a list of 'Truths I know about me' and the result was that she did figure out her WHY. It was about discovering the unique and differentiated talents of others, helping them to tap into it, and then harnessing the collected strengths of many diverse people and perspectives to achieve their full potential both as individuals and as a company. That is her WHY.

This WHY energises her, gives her purpose, helps her to work through the difficult situations and provides clarity that counteracts the occasional inertia.

We each need to find our WHY, our sense of purpose. This helps you to understand your comfort level with your career, personal choices and options, and the trade-offs you are prepared to make. It helps us to have the perspective to adjust to changing circumstances. Sometimes we make trade-offs consciously, sometimes unconsciously, and sometimes just intuitively. It helps to clearly articulate your strengths and trade-offs to yourself, and those around you.

If you have real career choices to make, you're already heading in the right direction, but, yes, making those career decisions can be challenging. It's about the level of risk you are prepared to take, your options, how others see you, and your own reality check about your strengths and the things you are not so good at. I am well into my fifth career (I did start out a long time ago) and some choices have been easier than others.

Luck can certainly come into it too: sometimes you can be lucky, sometimes not, and sometimes you will have to work at making your own luck.

First career choices: just a starting platform

Some people always have a sense of what they might want to do.

One of our sons, Patrick (aka Paddy) is a professional musician and music educator. His goal from about age nine was to be a jazz trumpeter—he announced this as soon as he picked up and started playing a trumpet.

When he was about thirteen, in his first year of high school, he had to write an essay about what he might want to do when he grew up. He wrote that, when he was in his mother's womb, he heard Louis Armstrong play trumpet and he knew then what he wanted to be.

While his teacher was quite concerned about the origins of his career choice, it made sense to us as his parents. And yes, being a jazz trumpeter is part of what he does today. But that clarity and follow-through is relatively rare.

When I was growing up there were generally two choices put to young women—teaching or nursing. I had always wanted to do teaching so that was fine with me at the time. I completed a Bachelor of Arts degree and then a Diploma of Education. My high school teaching 'methods', as they were called then, were History, English, Library Studies, and what was called 'New Media' in 1969. A few years later I also completed a course of study and exams to qualify as a professional librarian.

Unlike some of my school friends, I had parents who assumed that, if bright enough, I would go to university—though my parents both finished their formal schooling at fourteen. The very special thing about my parents was that they understood that each of their seven children were quite different. What was good for one of us, was not necessarily good for another. We were each encouraged to do what was right for us, and there was no pre-defined path. My eldest brother was the first of our generation to go to university, and all of us completed university studies, professional or technical training.

No matter your path, finding that sense of purpose and playing to your strengths helps you to navigate, redirect or expand your options when you hit those difficult inflection points in your career.

2

RISK: HOW MUCH ARE YOU PREPARED TO TAKE ON?

Making career choices: some safe, some very risky

Some of my career choices have been safe, but some have entailed a good level of risk.

In my work as an Executive Search Consultant we look for diversity in our candidates, some risk-taking, the extent executives and managers have been prepared to take on stretch roles, experienced very challenging situations or market conditions, or perhaps started a business, led a turnaround, or had to close one down.

My career might look at bit meandering to some. To me, it was always important to be growing and learning in a role. The initial threads were about education and managing information sources. This shifted over time to working with executives, initially in areas related to advising, coaching and coaxing. And later, leading services that did all those things.

I took on new roles as a bit of a stretch, and sometimes because they gave me the opportunity to do something I had not done before.

Let me share with you some of those career choices—the inherent risks that had to be assessed, and the career inflections they came to provide—so that you may hopefully gain some insight into the types of things that can occur, and to think about what direction you might have taken, given the same opportunities.

Generally, I stayed six or seven years in the one organisation taking on different or broader roles within it before moving on. It is really important to stay long enough to have built a solid track record of achievement, or in the words of a colleague of mine, 'To clean up the mess you might have made the first time around'.

Inflection number one: Ready for a stretch role

As General George Patton famously noted, 'Take calculated risks. That is quite different from being rash'.

I had quite deliberately remained in the teaching service throughout most of the 1970s, although I knew that there were other things I would want to do in time, in order to focus on having our four children and completing further study.

As chance would have it, while on that fourth short maternity leave after the birth of our daughter (following three sons), I received a call from the head office of the NSW Department of Education. Would I come in and have a discussion with them about a project they were planning? My name had been recommended to them as someone who might be able to provide them with some advice. They wanted to be able to capture a lot of the unpublished materials teachers were developing themselves, organise and make them available to others.

I realised about halfway through that this was a job interview. It was not a teaching role—it was creating a new information service from scratch, as the Department's first Curriculum Information Officer.

There were a few challenges inherent in this scenario: first, encouraging teachers to share their material; second, putting them into a form that could be shared (whatever that meant); then, providing some sort of readily accessible listing so other teachers knew what was available.

This was at a time when computers were at their most rudimentary, with no such thing as the sort of databases and searching capabilities that are available today, or even by the mid-1980s. This was over fifteen years before the most embryonic form of the Internet.

I mark it as my first experience of considered (calculated) career risk taking.

Re-use, rejig and redeploy

I like new roles, ones that no one has done before, that you can sort of make up as you go along. But the risk is that you can't really deliver what people are seeking, or you misjudge was that is.

I was able to employ a colleague to work with me, another teacher with graduate library qualifications whom I had met and thought would enjoy the challenge too. She was somewhat cautious.

I remember her asking me how we were going to figure this out. It was September and we were committed to delivering our product, whatever it was going to be, for the new school year in January.

My response was that I didn't really know but it was important and there must be a way. We would figure it out together, engage some others in a few brainstorms and workshops—and we did.

In the end, we delivered what was needed and probably more than what was expected: a guide and index to hundreds of unpublished curriculum materials across the two pilot regions in NSW—one metropolitan and one rural. It meant trips to Dubbo and Orange and other places to get buy-in from teachers, principals and bureaucrats.

We solved the technical issues through that age-old approach of looking at who had done something like this before. Don't re-invent—instead, re-use, rejig and redeploy.

Back then, the Australian Education Index was one of Australia's first 'databases' providing access to a range of materials. We convinced the head of that service, Margaret Findlay, to include our data in that index. Margaret was very obliging and, in fact, thrilled that we were using what she had developed.

Our service was duly launched and did well over about a sixteen-month period. But then politicians started to hear about it—that you could actually find out what was happening in schools at the classroom level. In the end this was seen as rather subversive and the service came under threat.

I have learned many times that good ideas sometimes threaten the way things are usually done, so they might then go through a pause phase, before their real value is realised five or ten years later. This is what happened to the Curriculum Information Project in NSW. It became the approach used nationally about seven years later.

Inflection number two: Taking on a real leadership role

Around this time we were moving our family to Melbourne in order for Robert to take up a new job—one that I had seen advertised and thought he was just right for. I had figured that at some stage we would move to Melbourne, as that is where his family was and his father was not well. We met at a student conference when we were each involved in the Students' Representative Councils – Robert in Melbourne at La Trobe University and me at Sydney. He had moved to Sydney to marry me but, for reasons I still find hard to fathom, he was not keen on Sydney's humidity. While, initially, the timing was not great, in the end it worked out quite well as it seemed like the innovative Curriculum Information Project, despite its success 'on the ground', was about to be put on hold.

In Melbourne, after a few months of freelancing and part-time work, I joined the teaching staff as a lecturer at what became RMIT University's Department of Information Services.

A few years later I was promoted to Senior Lecturer and, with the Head and my colleagues, led significant program and curriculum changes. We could see that components—and professional studies— of information, information technology, business information systems, library services and information management were starting to merge. Our programs needed rethinking and reworking—a task we accomplished with success.

Our Head of Department, Mike Ramsden, was made Acting

Dean for about eighteen months. This was about the same time that we had started renewing our programs. And while he was Acting Dean, I became Acting Head of Department.

I realised that if I was going to stay in academia for a while, I really needed to get a PhD, even if they were still unusual in the field in which I was working at the time. Somehow, amongst everything else, I thought I could fit that in. After all, I expected Mike would eventually resume the role of Head of Department, which would lighten my load, and that suited me just fine.

I asked one of my contacts at the University of Melbourne for advice regarding my PhD studies. He steered me in the direction of Melbourne Business School (MBS), where I presented my case to the Dean. I was eventually accepted as a part-time student, though there was no one on staff then who really had a background in what I wanted to do.

I learned many years later that my contact at the University of Melbourne also happened to be Chair of the Academic Board at the time. When he rang the Dean there, the assumption was that it would be a very good idea to accept me. Sometimes you can get lucky!

The day I received my acceptance papers from MBS was the same day that the Head called me in the evening to say that he had finally agreed to accept the role of Dean. All of us in the Department knew what that meant—whenever you lost your Head, you were without one for about eighteen months while someone conducted a review to see if the department and its programs were really needed.

So, when you are at your lowest ebb, without the most senior person, and most understaffed, you also have a very heavy review burden. Again, it was one of those decision points: should I apply for the Head's role when it became available in about a year's time? What would this mean for the PhD about which I had become very enthusiastic?

I did get a lot of encouragement from some unusual quarters— people I didn't know well who were keen for me to go for it and in the end I did. But first I decided I should hand over the Acting Head role to another likely internal candidate so he could have the opportunity to demonstrate his approach.

Meanwhile, I started planning a sabbatical, as the only way to kick-start my doctorate. After all I was a trained librarian so I knew how to do a literature search, and I would just have to figure out how to get things done over time.

I have given many workshops on how to do a PhD part-time when you have a lot of other things going on in your life. The secret is of course to outsource what you don't have to do, both at home and in your research.

But I have probably dissuaded, rather than persuaded, many people from doing a PhD, especially in what was the arcane British/ Australian model. What I always looked for in a PhD student is a real passion to investigate an area, someone who has a very good dose of discipline, and might have a supportive (enough) partner or environment. Completing a PhD is not essentially about being a smart person. It is about being persistent, with dogged determination, and researching an area that is absolutely fascinating to the one person that matters—yourself!

Outsource what you can

In deciding to pursue my PhD and concurrently take on the Head of Department role, I knew I might have finally taken on just too much. It was a ridiculously busy time—heading a department going through major changes, working on my PhD, co-parenting our four children (aged nine to sixteen when I took on the Head role) and of course managing multiple other relationships.

Back then, the first part of any PhD required a substantial literature search, which was later synthesised to create a great topic— or something the student would be prepared to spend the next few years researching.

My studies were relevant to what we were doing in the department, but we did not have funds to pay a researcher to assist with the leg work. After agreeing to lead a series of workshops with the Australian Institute of Management on Strategic Information Services, I was given approval to use the payment for these workshops to fund my literature searching. (Remember this was still before the Internet.) I approached one of the really good students, Carey Butler, to see if she was prepared to be my paid research assistant, and, fortunately, she said yes. I did the conceptual work and initial literature searching then Carey followed up on these, found the relevant articles, helped index things and generally gave me great support.

I also set the expectation that I would work from home most of each Tuesday, and I did. Sometimes I did catch-up work for the department, and other times I worked on the PhD.

My kids knew too that if they needed something attended to, a parent permission form signed or anything else like that, then that should be done before 8.30pm. From about 9pm to 11pm many nights I was working on the doctoral work, or sometimes other Departmental work.

But I was not sequestered away—to this day, my study just has a light Japanese screen instead of a door and is next to the kitchen.

Making that decision to get some help, or to outsource, is hard, but most people do say that, with hindsight, they should have done it sooner.

Share your challenges and ask for help

Always be willing to talk about what you are doing with others, to share some of the challenges, as you never know what might eventuate.

I took a few months sabbatical in the first year of the doctorate to travel, met other researchers in the US, and participated in some conferences. My data gathering included interviewing dozens of senior executives in Australia's major banks and it required some time to synthesise the findings. This led to the decision that I would need to take a few months off to complete the rest of the writing for the PhD. I was intending to take it as Leave Without Pay, which would also be a great incentive to get it done quickly.

However, one day I was discussing the timing dilemma with an acquaintance who had just been appointed to run a new commercially-focused research centre. He thought having me on his staff for a while would be a good thing as I understood what the centre was trying to achieve, had a relevant academic and professional background, and was part of a university with whom the centre was making linkages. We came to an agreement that I could spent eighty to eighty-five percent of my time on the PhD writing and about fifteen percent helping them get established. For that, he would pay almost my current salary. RMIT was happy about it as they had a link to the centre and so it was a bit of a win-win.

Getting the PhD done required discipline and drive. It also required an ability to compartmentalise what I was doing, which is something I have learned to do over time. It can be annoying to others as it means I might be overly focused and that level of persistence or focus can be off-putting or a bit of a mystery to others. People might call it selfish or self-centred, but I can live with that. After all, I had earlier supported Robert in many ways through his doctoral studies and, over many years, we have each supported each other to achieve what we wanted to do.

Many of the MBA students who have been in my classes have had similar experiences. If you have people to support and who need to support you, just figure out how you might get things done.

With open minds and wills it is amazing what can be jointly achieved.

3

DON'T BE AFRAID TO MOVE OUT OF YOUR COMFORT ZONE

Inflection number three:
Moving from a bureaucracy to entrepreneurship

As I was handing in swathes of my PhD thesis to Melbourne Business School, some of the MBS faculty started talking to me about possibly moving to join them. Technically, it would be a lower-level role than the one I had at RMIT, though the dollars would be similar. It would take me in quite a different direction but build on the doctoral work I was finishing.

It would be a big stretch again, as it would mean shifting my areas of teaching and taking on some new ones. At RMIT my major focus was teaching postgraduate students about management and leadership. At MBS it would be teaching MBA students about technology strategy and management. Also, MBS faculty were not offered tenure back then, which I had at RMIT. Instead, you were offered a two- or five-year contract. It tended to attract and build a cohort of academic staff who backed themselves and had very good links to the business community.

It would be another case of leaving a professional area where I had built a reputation, to take my career in a different direction and, in some ways, start all over again. But what mattered to me most was choosing the best long-term move in terms of my own learning. Which role had a bit more of a risky edge to it? Where would I be stretched and grow the most?

I chose the MBS option. It was a good move, but not without its challenging moments. The students generally had very high expectations of themselves and therefore for your contribution to that. Many were making considerable financial and personal sacrifices at key stages of their careers.

Moreover, MBS worked at pace that was a quantum faster than the then more bureaucratic RMIT. My role involved establishing a Key Centre for Technology Management and a new Master of Technology Management degree. What took five years to get started at RMIT took five months at MBS.

My colleague Peter Weill (now at MIT) and I did some ground-breaking research that investigated how organisations investing in technology-enabled business developments could get the most value from those developments.

I also learned that travelling for work is very stimulating as you have access to different people, businesses and a whole range of perspectives.

Inflection number four: Taking on a commercial Pty Ltd

In what turned out to be my seventh year at MBS (well, on my first tour of duty there), there were a number of career options opening up: I was being put forward to head the school's Executive Education, and also for a full Professorship. I also continued to get a number of invitations to consider working elsewhere, but I knew I did not want to work at any other business school—MBS was the best, at least in the Pacific region.

Peter and I grew our academic publication record, won an international Best Paper award, had an article coming out in the

Sloan Management Review, and a book under production with Harvard Business School Press.

I have learned over the years that I don't like to repeat things year after year. Once I have achieved my own goals, it is time to take on a different challenge. Certainly, leading Executive Education at MBS would be a big challenge, but I had also been approached a couple of times by the US-headquartered technology advisory services firm, Gartner Inc.

My initial response was that I did not want to work for an IT company. After all, I was not primarily a technologist—rather someone who was able to bridge the gap and bring business issues and technology capabilities together. I spoke enough of both languages to be useful at a time where there were few hybrids around.

Then Gartner approached me again with a different proposition and I had come to realise that Gartner was a professional services firm, not a technology company. This time the role was leading the relatively new Executive Program for Chief Information Officers in Australia. This meant moving fully into the commercial world, running a real P/L, working with sales people on business development, and being accountable for service delivery to some very senior executives.

Clearly, I was a risk for Gartner as there were a few things in there that I had not done before. In my conversations with the Gartner executives, I explained that we dealt with a group of client organisations at MBS. In fact, there were probably about forty globally who were participants in our research and development, and executive education.

For our part we shared our findings and insights with them as part of them providing access and/or funding. We ran many two- or three-day executive education programs, our favourite being 'IT for non-IT executives', which was sometimes funded by one of the technology firms. And our centre certainly had a budget, which had to balance, and revenue and expense streams. But those were rather basic statistics.

Heading to Gartner was a risk for me too.

I would again be leaving an environment where I had built up a strong reputation, both locally and internationally, to go to the 'dark side'; that is, commercially focused research, which had different drivers and balance. The research had to focus closely on what would resonate with clients, and not so much on what we thought was important (though, in our case, the fit was usually good anyway).

Both roles, Executive Education at MBS and the Gartner role, came to a head at the same time. I took half a day off to sit at home and think about what I really wanted to do. I drew up a one-page business plan for the first twelve months in each role, and overlaid this with the usual questions: 'Which is a bigger stretch?' and 'Where will I learn more?'

Gartner was the definite winner, but it was hard to share with my colleagues and more than challenging to explain to the Dean.

At that stage, Gartner was not a name known by many business people, even though I tried to explain that it was 'the McKinsey of the IT Advisory world'. After some further negotiations though, I did leave to take on the next career challenge.

Build on existing capabilities

MBS had enabled me to build a base of capabilities for the future. Again, the role I was going to was a new role that I could shape—I hoped!

An acquaintance once commented to me about my career moves, 'Somehow what you do is build on your capabilities and experiences in a way that gives you future options. You didn't know what they were, but when the timing was right an opportunity came along and you took it'.

The hardest part was leaving valued colleagues and young students whose optimism often knew no bounds, and who were generally challenging and stimulating to work with.

It was also hard to tell my parents. They were proud of their daughter as an academic, considering their lack of formal education. I made a special trip to Sydney to explain to them the new challenge

I was taking on. My mother was devastated and my father confused. It was only when I explained that if it didn't work out I would always be welcome back as an academic that their concerns were somewhat lessened.

For the family it meant a lot more travel for me, but we probably didn't realise just how much till well after I started. I also had some trouble explaining to the kids exactly what my role was. They could understand being a professor, but how could they explain this new role to their friends?

When I returned to MBS many years later, they breathed a sigh of relief, I think, as they could more easily understand and explain the nature of my work.

The challenge of repetition

I spent the next six years at Gartner moving into progressively broader regional, then global, roles. It was a fantastic experience, and, as expected, I learned a lot.

For many years I believed I had about the best job in the world—developing new and valued services, working with smart and collaborative colleagues, visiting clients in different countries and learning more about the diversity of industries, firms, and government agencies that I would have thought possible.

But in my sixth year at Gartner I started to feel that my role was becoming a bit repetitive. I had suggested to the then CEO and executive a number of other roles I could do, or businesses we could expand on. However, I was usually told something like, 'No, we need you to keep doing what you are doing. You do it well and we can't afford for you to do something else'.

Be wary about using the phrase 'We need you to keep doing what you do' with a valued employee. They are trying to tell you that they need to do something different, no matter how much you want them to continue doing the same role.

When it came time to start working on the next annual survey of CIO issues and attitudes I found myself saying, 'Here we go again'. This triggered some reflection over the next few months about what I really wanted to do next.

I did not do any active looking, but I had a number of concurrent offers. One was a lucrative role working with a competitor and being based fully in the US. I went through the process, was offered a role and then realised I really didn't want to be domiciled outside Australia. We might have done it some years earlier, but there were too many things now back in Melbourne that were important to us.

Paul Rizzo and Ian Harper at MBS had contacted me about returning to the school as Associate Dean and leading what is now called the Senior Executive MBA. I would be able to devote a day or more a week to consulting and applied research and, thus, rebuild those local connections that I had not spent much time on. I accepted this role.

I gave Gartner about four months' notice, so that my successor could be revealed at the same time as the public announcement of my departure, and returned to MBS to lead both the academic and marketing roles of the Senior Executive MBA.

Working with mature executives in an intense program meant that you were often explaining how things needed to work to people who were used to being in charge of their organisation or line of business.

Quite a few found it difficult to return to this type of study—in four residential four-week blocks—over a period of about sixteen months. No matter how we explained to them that they would need to hand over the reins of their business role to someone else while doing a four-week module, some did not believe it till part-way through.

Meanwhile, I was proud that the team that I had grown and developed at Gartner continued to be regarded as high performers and remained largely intact for quite a few years.

4

GRASP BIG CHANGE MANAGEMENT OPPORTUNITIES

Inflection number five:
Co-leading a major business turnaround

About ten months into my time at MBS I had a number of interesting phone calls with Gartner.

The previous CEO had left about midyear and the incoming CEO had spent some time investigating why a big chunk of the business was stagnating (which was also contributing to a low and sluggish share price).

Clearly a turnaround was required. Feelers had been put out to a small number of people and I was one of them.

I had maintained quite close links with Gartner while at MBS. Gartner is an iconic company and, like MBS, an organisation that once you have worked there, you will always have continuing ties.

During my last six months at MBS, the book I had co-authored at Gartner, *The New CIO Leader,* was on its way to the printer, and due to be launched at the next three major Gartner Symposia in Orlando, Cannes and Sydney.

I was invited to meet with the newish Gartner CEO, Gene Hall, at the Cannes symposium. His first words were that he wanted me back in the company. I replied that that might be possible, provided I could continue living in Melbourne.

This time the challenge was of a different type. The business that I had been part of previously represented about one fifth of Gartner's total revenue, while the stagnating Research part of the business represented more than three quarters of total revenue.

My friend and former boss Robin Kranich had been asked to lead the business turnaround of the Research business, and my new role was to lead new product development as part of that turnaround. We all knew that most of the new Research business products that had been launched in the previous four or five years had faltered, and that the product portfolio needed an overhaul.

That challenge and opportunity was too good to refuse, though it again came with quite a few trade-offs.

Taking risks leads to learnings

If you have the chance to work on a major turnaround, start a new business, or lead a risky project, take it! These opportunities don't come up very often. No matter how it turns out, you will learn a huge amount along the way.

I had made it clear at the outset that if I did return to Gartner I would stay until we did the turnaround, which would probably be about three or four years at most.

I sort of squared things away with my husband Robert when I returned to Australia from Cannes. He had come to enjoy seeing more me than he had for some years, but he also knew this was a great opportunity and that it was the sort of role I would probably relish.

Now I just had to explain to the new MBS Dean, who had started in November, that I would be leaving. He was gracious and agreed that I could leave in the new year after we put a few other developments in place—inducting a new group of students in October and planning for the revised international module, which included time in China.

My advice to him, though, was that the workload really needed additional staffing. I knew that none of the current academic staff would take on both the academic and marketing leadership as I had done, and that turned out to be the case.

Additional staffing was put in place for the next program leaders and my role became two roles after my departure.

A different kind of return

The return to Gartner as Senior Vice President for New Product Development was both gratifying and a bit scary.

A group of the often-tetchy senior analysts told me the fact that I had seen fit to return meant that I must have thought we could turn the business around. That in turn, had a considerable, if concerning, impact on me. If they thought we could do this, then I really did have to believe we could, and that we would. It was a kind of positive re-enforcement and challenge rolled into one.

I did have to rethink how I did things quite early on. I was much more accustomed to working with a group who would think conceptually through a problem and work through to a solution. I quickly learned in this new role, that I always had to start with the numbers that could possibly be achieved through a particular course of action, no matter how fuzzy those numbers might be.

It was a crash course in remembering to shape and present the case in the style of the recipients—not the way that seemed most logical and obvious to me. This was something that I did know, but had to remember to do all the time. And, after one not-so-good 5am conference call, I learned to make sure the rhythm of the work meant that I was in Gartner's US Headquarters for all the critical meetings.

After about eighteen months, we started to see a real turnaround in our numbers and I knew it was probably time to think about the next chapter in my career. Other people had 'got it' and were now running with the new products and services. I was under pressure to move to the US, but did not want to. And I missed spending a lot of time with clients, which is where and how I gain a lot of energy.

Sometime prior, I had been approached by, but declined joining, executive search firms. Their business models meant that, as a partner, you were effectively in competition with your colleagues. For better or worse, I have the collaborative 'gene', which better suited academia and Gartner-type roles.

Through this time period, I kept in touch with Mark Lelliott, Managing Partner at a leading search firm and then through his leadership of other businesses. We worked together on a major global Gartner report on what makes executives successful: he led from the executive search firm, and a colleague and I co-led this for Gartner. After that, I provided some feedback about capability and assessment tools he and his colleagues had developed.

When he approached me about being a candidate for a role in a large merger and acquisition he was working on, I asked, 'Why me?' For someone who I thought didn't know me all that well, I found the answer fascinating.

He described some attributes I had not really thought about, such as my ability to diagnose what was happening in organisations, the value of experience in working with diverse executive teams, and my ability to provide a level of clarity through understanding the essence of a situation, making complex things simpler to understand. I just hadn't thought of these as particular attributes, nor had I realised how generically useful they might be!

Regular self-assessment is a good habit to develop. Why regular? The biggest disadvantage of assessing yourself is that it is difficult to be objective about both your strengths and weaknesses. By making a habit of self-assessment you are more attuned to picking up on the feedback from others, which can realign your perceptions.

Inflection number six: Embarking on yet another new career

At one of my occasional lunches with Mark during 2006, he made some comments about how perhaps working with him and the team at what became EWK International (and later NGS Global) would be a good move. I thought he was just being polite and didn't take too much notice.

Later that afternoon, though, I started to think things through. Perhaps it was time for my next career change.

I had indicated to my Gartner colleagues that I would only stay until we turned the business around and clearly that was happening. I rang Mark back later that afternoon and asked him if he was actually offering me a job? The response was of course he was, and how could I not realise that immediately.

Over the next few months, during discussions with the executive search partners, I learned why they might want me to join them, and why and how I could succeed in leadership advisory and executive search work.

My experience as an executive educator and advisor, executive professional services roles, and leading product development seemed to be a very good combination from their viewpoint.

Their business model was quite different from most competitors. It was (and is) a very collegial and collaborative model. They were all mature and experienced. It was the partners that played the predominant role in both bringing in business and in doing the execution of that business. There was not a layer of associates to whom they passed on the bulk of the work with clients. Sure, they had researchers, but partners doing the work was a key part of value proposition.

I took my usual approach and thought through where I would learn most, where I figured I would make the best contribution, and then, being in the second half of my 50s, asked myself what was likely to provide the best platform for the next ten or so years of my career?

We agreed that for the first six weeks my focus was to review all the intellectual property the group had developed and to put that into a more 'industrial' or 'reusable' form. The expectation was that it would take six months or more for me to be fully 'inducted' into this new business and I was grateful for that.

However, things usually don't work out quite as planned and this was the case here too. I did focus heavily on the IP work, but also spent some time with clients alongside my colleagues and then brought in some early work.

On my second day I went with a colleague to have a discussion with a potential client. We left with two searches confirmed, and I thought, 'How easy was that?'

The answer was that it was the result of a relationship built over time, and not to assume that most or many meetings would result like that. Over the next ten years I had many lessons.

5

PARENTING OFTEN REQUIRES TRADE-OFFS

Different stages lead to different choices

We regularly need to make choices about our next steps without knowing what is ahead. This means being flexible, adaptable and keeping our long-term options open.

It might be that an elderly parent needs more attention, a sibling is having difficulties and needs more support, or you want more time with your growing children.

Sometimes you will make trade-offs consciously, sometimes unconsciously, and sometimes just intuitively. It helps if those trade-offs are clearly articulated to yourself and those around you.

In Executive Search work we are constantly contacting people about their next potential career opportunity. We live every day with candidates, or potential candidates, weighing up the level of disruption they might want to cause their families by moving interstate or moving to a new country, or their colleagues by leaving.

Moving to a new role can create a whole set of new demands, particularly in the first few months when you are working to get your head around what is expected, dealing with a new environment and, sometimes, a new industry. Maybe, it might just not be the right time.

It's helpful to take the longer view on your career, and sometimes to 'hasten slowly' and stay where you are for a while, as it suits your current circumstances.

Company director and board chair Kathryn Fagg started her career as an engineer on oil and gas rigs in Bass Strait. She later moved to management consulting with McKinsey, and then had senior executive roles with ANZ Banking Group and BHP Steel/ BlueScope. She emphasises the need to clarify what is important to yourself, your family and to your employer. Be clear about what you can do and about the ground-rules.

There will always be trade-offs on both the career and home fronts. Decide what they are, what can work, and then get on with it.

You can have it all, just not necessarily at the same time

While the sentiment that 'you can have it all, just not at the same time' has been credited recently to Oprah Winfrey, I first heard it stated more than ten years ago by Jude Munro, the then Chief Executive of Brisbane City Council (one of the largest municipalities in the world). She was addressing a cross-section of executives about the approaches the Council was taking to ensure they had a sufficiently diverse workforce, and that they did not lose good people who could otherwise be better supported through family-friendly policies and practices.

Her willingness to articulate that she knew we all had to make different choices at different times, that working for BCC was not an end in itself, was refreshing, particularly at the time. I made a conscious decision to stay in a career in my 20s that suited my circumstances. At the time, teaching gave me a bit of flexibility to take on further study while also managing a growing family.

We women have the wombs so, for now, on average, we are more likely to take a bit more time out than men. But who knows what will happen in time, and already significant numbers of men and women are making decisions that mean each of them, at some stage, will work in paid employment less than full-time.

Seeing this more shared engagement of both men and women, and same sex couples, with their families today is just terrific. It opens up the options to parents much more than has been the case in the past.

Becoming a parent can result in different skills

Having to be accountable for the care and wellbeing of others— children, a parent or another family member—forces us to exercise, or uncover, our abilities to prioritise, make trade-offs, ask for assistance, and delegate.

Alisa Bowen is a digital leader who has worked for many years at the nexus of digital consumer technologies and business model disruption inside traditional media organisations. Today she is based in Los Angeles as an international technology executive for the Disney organisation. She is aware that she has always been something of a workaholic and earlier in her career she had difficulty trusting others to do their jobs well.

She was used to working in male-oriented environments. It was with some fear and dread quite a few years ago that she told her boss she was pregnant with her first child. She was concerned about how she would balance everything and keep up her performance if she could not work eighteen hours a day, six days a week.

She was surprised with the reaction of her boss, which went something like, 'This baby will be the making of your executive leadership, because you will just simply have to delegate. And you'll learn for yourself that sheer hard work is not enough. You will have to work smarter, not harder, to keep advancing.'

Alisa notes that her boss was one hundred percent correct and that is when she began to focus more on building teams and networking based on meaningful connections and relationships. She wishes that she had learned earlier on that life is not a sprint but a marathon.

Alisa later came to realise that as her children got older they often needed their parents more—for spiritual guidance, academic support, discipline and emotional involvement.

These things can't easily be outsourced but, with her demanding travel schedule, at least Facetime, WeChat or Skype allows a parent to have some form of regular presence, if not there in person.

Trade-offs need to be made at different stages

Having one parent take a career pause or a role that is less demanding in terms of constant availability has been common for women, but not as much for men.

It usually comes about from a good discussion on how to get things done, how to identify different priorities and what timely trade-offs need sacrificing.

Taking the 'foot off the career pedal' is the description that J.P. Morgan's Lalitha Biddulph uses to describe how she and her husband Ross approached making choices when their children were under five years old.

They decided that Lalitha was experiencing considerable 'career runway' so Ross took three years out of the workforce and then returned to work part-time for the following five years. They believed this approach was important to ensure that their children had the values they believed would be important to them.

Glenys Beauchamp, Secretary/CEO of the Australian Department of Health, took nine years out when her three children were young and doesn't regret this at all. At the time she had to resign rather than take leave. It meant that when she rejoined the paid workforce, she took a role considerably more junior than the one she had left nine years before, and also had to rebuild her personal confidence.

As her career re-ignited, she and her husband made choices that included his career then taking a back seat, so that one partner was always able to have more time with their three children.

Christine Kilpatrick, Chief Executive Officer at Melbourne Health, shared that, earlier in her career, she and her husband invested heavily in nannies so she could return to work within a couple of months. Her view is that if you stay out of the workforce for too long, it is too hard to get back in. She says it's important to have a career that suits you and you never know what lies ahead.

That period of taking time out, for women and men, has a different impact depending on the nature of career and work.

For early or mid-career academics, a break can have a greater impact than many other areas.

Jane Den Hollander, the Vice-Chancellor of Deakin University from 2012 to 2019, instituted a new program to address that issue.

While on maternity leave, staff at Deakin were allowed to have a research assistant in order to keep their work progressing. This meant that when they returned to full-time, academics were able to continue more easily, rather than from a dead stop. Their research had continued, and there were publications in the pipeline. This made a world of difference and kept gifted academics in the profession.

The right child-minding arrangements require persistence

Where there are babies and children involved, learn to embrace the ensuing chaos.

We took our first child each morning, from the age of about five months, to the home of a woman who turned out to be a children's book author. It was a bit chaotic, but she loved kids, and I am sure fed his imagination wonderfully.

Returning to work four months after our second child was born was more problematic. Just as I thought it was not going to be possible, we came upon a wonderful Scottish woman, Dinah, and her husband, Bill.

Our kids went to her home for the next seven years. It did mean of course that when our second son, Andrew, started school and referred to his 'wee little case' that we were asked how long we had lived in Scotland.

When I had that interview for the Education Headquarters role mentioned earlier, the Division Head knew I was on maternity leave, so asked me a question that was along the lines of, 'How will you manage coming back to work after the birth of your first baby?' Returning from maternity leave, let alone taking on such a role, was not the norm in the late 1970s.

What he did not realise was that it would in fact be the fourth time I would be returning to work from maternity leave.

My response was something like, 'Well the first week or two will be dreadful and I will wonder why on earth I am doing this, by the third or fourth week I might have sorted a few things out, and by about week eight I will start to get into a rhythm'.

He was a bit taken aback and I think almost withdrew the job offer. But I told him it was fine, and I was sure I could help him solve the curriculum information issue, if he could leave the family situation to Robert and me to work through.

Kathryn Fagg and her husband made the decision early on to enlist a full-time nanny. While this was something they could afford at the time, it was still a stretch. This enabled a good level of stability and routine, particularly as their nannies stayed for long periods.

Managing as a single parent

Where there is one parent or carer rather than two, challenges are much greater.

Jody Evans, Associate Dean at MBS became a single parent when she was six months pregnant. Her son is now ten years old and, as she puts it, 'literally grew up at the Business School'.

She has been reluctant to tell people how to juggle career and parenting as there is, of course, no one right way. But, she shared with me that her approach is to include her son in everything she does, not seeking that allusive notion of balance—rather combining her two worlds as much as possible.

Her son sat in classes while she taught, saw her present at industry events, travelled with her for research projects and played

Lego at her feet while she finished writing papers at home.

He now talks with pride about what his mum does and understands why she travels and is out quite a few evenings. As Jody explains, 'The more he understands what I do and why I do it, the less guilty I feel when I have to spend time away'.

I always like to set expectations for parents returning to work after leave that their arrangements are likely to be less than perfect, that things will be difficult and messy, but their kids will undoubtedly survive and that they have the wonderful advantage of experiencing the company of other caring adults and other children.

Kids have views on the experience too

Our three sons always seemed to think everything I did was normal and they didn't mind that I was never at tuckshop or missed a few important events.

Early on, and in her early teens, our daughter Katie was a bit more concerned and adopted my Melbourne-based sister Michelle as her surrogate mum at school. At least her aunt was around and did tuckshop duties, as Michelle had a daughter at the same school.

In her early years of high school Katie announced that she would not go back to work after having children, that she thought she would want to stay at home and be a full-time carer. I told her that was perfectly fine if that was what she wanted to do.

When she was studying for the HSC, there was a component about maternal deprivation in one of her psychology classes. The teacher was apparently quoting the old Bowlby studies quite inappropriately.

Katie told us she was incensed. She promptly stood up in class and challenged the teacher to indicate what was wrong with her (Katie)—after all, her mother and father had always worked in paid employment outside the home. She went to home-based day care and then to a crèche from about two and half years of age. What in particular was wrong with her and what were the signs, in her, of deprivation?

I gather the teacher was a bit stunned and might have taught that section differently after that.

Katie's position about being a full-time carer did change over time. In her late thirties she is now more like me than either of us might ever have imagined. She and her husband have two young boys and they both work full-time, but they have sought some flexibility in their arrangements. This enables them to be actively engaged parents with full-time work commitments.

We each have to figure out how we can best blend parenting and working full-time, if that is what we want to do. It is a matter of working through what trade-offs make sense to you and being comfortable with that. Enjoy what you do and thrive with your choices. Just remember how lucky you are if you have choices, as many people don't have that luxury.

6

DECIDE YOUR COURSE AND EXORCISE THE GUILT THING

Avoid decision remorse

When you make your choices, the worst thing you can do is to feel bad about them, or to keep regretting them. Your demeanour can and will impact those around you.

It helps to do whatever you can to minimise any tendencies towards perfectionism and to work out what you DON'T need to do. Setting expectations of those around you, at home and at work, is also important.

When she was a business executive in NAB, Lisa Gray (now CEO of the Victorian Funds Management Corporation) made sure that matters such as parent/teacher meetings at her children's school were clearly marked in her calendar. They were initially entered in there by her then assistant as something like 'external business meeting'. She changed that to clearly mark it as a parent meeting at the school as she wanted to set the example that it was okay to take a few hours out from time to time to attend to family matters.

Abigail Bradshaw started her career as a military lawyer and has spent the past five years in London and Canberra as a public servant in national security portfolios. She and her husband had many discussions about how to manage their different work and family demands. In the end they hired an au pair. At first they felt this was indulgent, but they came to the view that it was the best thing they ever did for themselves and their kids. It took the stress out of the beginning and end of each day and meant more peaceful, quality family time.

Yes, you do need to have the right partner (a REALLY important choice to make). It helps too to bring your kids up to be independent and confident individuals. Our four all learned to cook and clean, to take responsibility for themselves and to contribute to the running of the household. To this day, one of our sons is the fastest and best sandwich maker around. Another always has the most beautifully ironed shirts, when this is necessary.

Perfect is the enemy of good

As Gartner's Robin Kranich puts it, 'You don't have to do it all. It's about picking your spots and knowing that perfect is the enemy of good. Your ability to give yourself permission to lower some standards so you can preserve emotional capital is a gift'.

Until after the birth of our fourth child, we did all the housework ourselves. This was not because we were particularly virtuous or enjoyed it. It was more of a financial necessity and we could manage doing it.

However, when heading back to work for that interesting full-time role in Education Headquarters, we discussed getting a cleaner in for a few hours once a week. Apart from the demands of our work and kids, I suffer from hay fever so cleaning for a couple of hours meant I wasn't able to do anything but sneeze for the rest of the day. Besides two of the kids were now in primary school and the demands of weekend sports and music commitments were making their presence felt.

Robert wasn't keen to have someone else come into our home, but in the end, I just organised it. It gave us back a bit more time and made my Saturdays more enjoyable. And Robert never regretted it either!

When our boys were in the later years of high school and early years of university, each of them successively took on the paid role of house cleaner. It was not a difficult job, they could do it at a time that suited and they had good supervision. Each of them did a good job.

We did offer the job to Katie when our youngest son went off to do other things, but she declined. She had already organised paying jobs that were more aligned to her career goals.

Our kids also learned a few other skills along the way. Katie attributed some of her formidable social skills to her experiences with the Australian Children's Choir through high school.

She loved the choir and singing and wanted to join more of their specialist groups. The problem was that rehearsals were about eight kilometres from our home, with no easy public transport access. One of us could usually pick her up in the evening but getting her there by 6pm was a challenge.

The deal became that if she could find another family who could get her there, we would bring her and the other chorister home. This meant that on her first rehearsal she always had to find out where everyone lived and then negotiate some car pool arrangements.

She was good at this and I don't think she missed any sessions in which she really wanted to participate.

Don't make a habit of bringing home gifts

In all my travelling for work I never felt obliged to bring home a gift for our children as a matter of course. If I saw a T-shirt or a CD or something that one of our four children would love, I might buy it. But that didn't mean I bought something for the other three.

Our kids understood that (I think!). I am aghast when women or men rush around buying presents on work trips. What this often conveys is that idea that, 'I am away therefore I am being neglectful/ not a good parent. I am buying you something to compensate for that and make me feel better'.

Often all it does is set up a situation where your kids expect to be compensated because you are doing what your role requires. My perspective was to get them accustomed to the way the world works.

Having said that, I should add that my frequent commitments to be at Gartner Headquarters in Stamford, Connecticut, meant regular trips to New York City, a 45-minute commuter train ride away.

This often meant a weekend afternoon pouring over the stock at the iconic and rambling Colony Music store near Times Square. Many (many) dollars were spent in that store over the years for two children in particular—one who is the professional musician (trumpeter) and music teacher, and the other who is a performer, music theatre actor and musician.

The Colony Music staff there were the human embodiment of what Amazon does today, 'If you like this then you will like that'.

I would sometimes arrive with a list from the two performers in the family and the staff would be impressed with my knowledge and taste for the latest in jazz and Broadway or off-Broadway's 'hot' new songwriter/musical team. Maybe that was partly why the kids were ever so understanding of their mother's wanderings.

Our kids knew that someone might get something that Mum had seen and thought was a good idea at the time, but they would not all get presents just because I had been away doing my job.

When travelling for work, enjoy the surrounds

One of my other insights was that, if you travel, don't rush home with things half-done. Stay another day, or whatever it takes to arrive home with the work done so you can be fully present (at least for a while) or take some downtime. Go visit a gallery or museum, walk around whatever city you are in to soak up the atmosphere, go do some shopping, watch a play or a sports game. If you do that you are more likely to be more relaxed as well as more interesting to talk to when you get home!

I have to confess that Robert was not fully aware of this policy of mine until quite recently. A couple of years ago, I led one of those lunchtime sessions with a 'Women in Technology' group. Also on the platform was a Human Resources Executive of one of Australia's largest companies. After I made my comments about the value of taking some downtime, she came up to me to thank me for the advice and told me she was going back to the office to redo her schedule for her London trip the following week to include an extra day out.

She ran into Robert and me in the foyer at an event a little while later, where she commented to Robert that he was clearly a very understanding person. I then had a little bit of explaining to do.

As a friend of mind is fond of saying, 'Not everyone has to know everything all the time'.

The caveat:
we each have different drivers, different comfort levels

Each of us is different. My purpose here is to illustrate how we deal with ourselves, using some of my journey, and that of some other women, to provide context and learnings.

I don't expect others to copy the way I have approached things, and I expect not many would want to!

As Jody Evans indicated, there is no one right way. We each find ourselves in different circumstances, we were brought up differently, have varied experiences and different levels of tolerance for ambiguity and stress. What is really important is for each of us to understand our own motivations and strengths and play to those.

The leading Company Chairman and Director, Elizabeth Proust put it this way, 'Women need to work with each other, build great networks, take a few career risks, and also ensure that at least one domestic skill is a major deficiency. Mine is cooking. I don't and won't cook'.

7

KNOW AND PLAY TO YOUR STRENGTHS

Be realistic about your strengths and experience

Reflecting on what has, and has not, worked for you previously can give you useful information about your strengths, limitations and development needs.

What roles did you really enjoy and why, or what parts of your current role do you really enjoy and do well?

Working with a large corporate firm about four years ago, a colleague and I were having a feedback session with an ambitious young executive who reported in two levels below the CEO. Let's say his name was Ahmed.

Ahmed was desperate for the next level role, and, unbeknown to us, had just missed out on that role for the second time in three years.

At the end of the session he asked straight-out did we think he would ever obtain that role, or one just like it? To date, no one had really explained to him why he had been unsuccessful—twice.

Our response, in a respectful but direct manner, went something like this, 'Well if you spend years developing a few particular areas, and then turn yourself inside out and become a different person, maybe you might get there. But why would you want to do that?'

He was a bit stunned and we then had a more measured discussion about his real strengths and where these—plus his great experiences—could take him. Three years later he continued to use his attributes well in an expanded role in the same firm, but not in the type of role to which he originally aspired. And he is quite okay with that.

You should seek this sort of feedback on your own skill set. It might come from your boss, colleagues, those you lead or your clients, customers or other stakeholders. It could come through a formal 360-degree process, or thoughtful feedback and interactions with your friends and family. Hopefully it comes from all of those sources.

Invest in your development

Self-awareness about your strengths, together with your limitations (euphemistically called your development needs), provides the basis of your personal development and investment plan.

Where can your strengths, capabilities and attributes be deployed most appropriately? Are there areas that really matter? Which one or two areas, with a small investment, will make an exponential impact on your contribution, job satisfaction, or your options? Know what areas don't matter so much and accept that these are not your strengths, nor are they likely to be, and so be it.

Part two examines what you should be doing in relation to those you lead and manage. For now, let's focus on you.

Many years ago, a fellow panel member, Bob Bisdee, gave me a coffee mug at an industry conference. Bob was a careers counsellor for many years and the motto Bob had on those mugs was 'steer your own career'. I kept that mug for many years as something of a reminder, as I thought it was very good advice.

Christine Kilpatrick began her career as a medical intern and resident, before a rotation in neurology convinced her to become a neurologist. She later became the Chief Medical Officer at Melbourne Health where she realised that, despite her somewhat extensive medical experience, in order to truly gain the credibility she needed for that role, and to become a CEO, she had to invest in an MBA.

A decade or two ago, people working in large organisations or government agencies would expect the organisation to take the initiative in development opportunities for them.

Organisations do need to invest in their people, but the most effective development takes place in those that are attuned to benefit from it—those with a strong orientation to accept responsibility for their own development and invest in it.

Professional development, formal and informal, and professional engagement, has always been a key part of my DNA. It has brought me into contact with some fabulous people throughout my career.

In the work I do today, it is something we look for in those we are working with. I am always amazed at those who seem to get by without this form of stimulation and commitment. They just don't know what they are missing—until it is too late.

Self-development is your responsibility

These days, most employees get that self-development is their responsibility too.

It's always been something I've prioritised. In the 1970s I developed an early interest in how computers could be applied to indexing and making documents more readily available. This might not sound too exciting to some, but a whole new world was opening up—not much was happening on this front in the school system at the time, but things were starting to develop in local government libraries.

My local library at Ryde in Sydney was an early mover. While on maternity leave for child number four, I approached them about the possibility of working a day or two a week to understand how this all worked and to gain some experience to take into the education sector.

They were delighted with my interest and employed me two days a week (on a somewhat nominal salary). It turned out to be a great investment as, later, when I was asked to head that NSW Education project I was comfortable about my ability to work out what might be needed.

We have worked in organisations where individuals who, when invited to come forward and indicate where they saw their contribution being of most value during a major change in their company, seemed unable to respond.

They stubbornly indicated they did not know, as they had not seen the new organisation chart. What a wasted opportunity! Their response said a huge amount about their attitude and it was noted.

In the same organisation, in a co-design session, some of the early career managers were working with us on the capabilities that were important for future managers. We had used the words 'ongoing professional development' in one of the capabilities about their learning orientation. It was an organisation where courses were available and sometimes people were 'allocated' to them. The managers discussed this for a while and then suggested we change the wording to be 'self-initiated professional development'. In their view, that is what distinguished those who really took accountability for themselves and who were able to get others to accept accountability. They took accountability for their own learning and did not expect things to be handed to them.

Share your aspirations to progress your career

Earlier in her career, company director Kathryn Fagg made it clear to her then employer, ANZ Banking Group, that though she came to the bank in a strategy and project role, she was keen to move to a significant line role.

She had come from consulting with McKinsey, but knew that to progress her career a line role was critical. She initially led the retail bank in two smaller states, and then was appointed as General

Manager of 5000 employees at the retail bank in New Zealand.

She later accepted the role of President of Asia for BlueScope Steel. There were some trade-offs in the move, but the opportunity to lead a business across multiple geographies in fast-moving markets was stimulating and rewarding. It also built her capacities for cultural understanding, taking in different points of view and perspectives, as well as compassion and tolerance.

In working with a number of groups of executives and managers, I have been struck by different attitudes to diversity in careers.

When an organisation is seeking individuals who can do things differently it can be hard to find them internally if a large percentage of staff have never worked anywhere else, or if they have not been sufficiently curious about how work gets done elsewhere.

The challenge is less if your organisation is large with many different components. You might have been able to experience multiple ways of doing things in different types of businesses or services. But if it is just large with the same or similar processes, products or services in every area, then it can be challenging to think really innovatively or tackle a problem in a completely different way.

Get the balance right

In a recent address to the Institute of Public Administration Australia, Heather Smith, Secretary/CEO of the Australian Department of Jobs and Small Business, noted that much of the Australian Public Service had only ever worked in one department.

Such lack of diversity was not helpful, as it likely meant that people had not experienced different contexts, different ways of problem solving and different ways of thinking.

Not long ago, I was in a conversation with a well performing manager (let's call her Janine) about some options her organisation had offered her. She had worked in the IT group in two large organisations in her twenty-five-year career, in application roles and as a senior Program Director. She reported to the Chief Information

Officer. Her dilemma was that she was being offered a line role
running a customer service centre and her initial reaction was
to decline this opportunity, as it would take her away from her IT
career. I had a different reaction, seeing it as a great opportunity and
one that, after some due diligence, she should grab with open arms.
We were each surprised at the other's reactions.

I was again reminded of my clients' demands for the breadth of
experiences that demonstrate adaptability and problem solving.

Consider: How diverse has your career been to date? Have
you had the opportunity to go into new or different areas in your
organisation, or in another organisation? What did you learn from
that? How has it informed the way you look at situations? To what
extent do you have multiple lenses to look at problems, or different
types of experiences to provide you with a broader context for action?

Getting the balance right can be a challenge. Make sure each
movement progresses or broadens your experience base, rather than
repeating the same experiences.

And, of course, too much moving around can mean that you
never get to experience the fallout from what you have commenced
or partially implemented. You may get a reputation for not staying
around to deal with the reality of implementation.

In a nine-year period, three years each in three different roles is
usually better for your career, learning and development than four
or five.

Diversity can be a career differentiator

A key differentiator of the leaders and managers we place is the
diverse nature of their experience.

Over past years, my colleagues and I have developed and
assessed candidate pools for many roles in the public, not-for-
profit and commercial sectors. We've also looked at the capabilities
and development needs of many hundreds of individuals for talent
management and succession planning.

What we, and our clients, look for is variety of experience built on curiosity and enough depth in one area that might have been gained in the first seven or eight years of a career. For example: where has Janine or Charlie or Gordon gone outside his or her comfort zone and really stretched him or herself? Where did they take a calculated risk in their career and back themselves? What is the spread of their domain and industry experience? How close have they really been to their constituency whether it be citizens, customers or consumers?

It is hard to be a credible candidate for a senior role, in any area, without some diversity of experience. For example, a key element of the succession planning we have worked on is whether the background of individual executives and managers has real breadth in both strategy or policy shaping, and strategic execution.

While you don't have to be fabulous at both, being great at one and having a reasonable level of competence in the other makes for a well-rounded manager or aspiring executive.

In the public sector, we often see senior public servants who have moved from state government to federal government, who are great at service delivery but who need some rounding in the policy area. This might be gained from a well-designed period of eighteen to twenty-four months in a central agency. The reverse is also true.

We have worked with Secretaries, Directors-General and CEOs to provide operational experience for some whose background has been in the policy domain to the virtual exclusion of operational and real service delivery experience.

Of course, this needs to be done in a thoughtful, deliberate and risk-managed way. The benefits, though, have been significant.

Seek out some character-building experiences

If it looks like your background might be a bit too narrow, then it might be time to be proactive about expanding your experiences— either inside or outside your current organisation.

Working for a large internationally focused organisation, or the public sector, might expose you to different areas, geographies, cultures and projects. Or, you might have had the opportunity to be seconded to a supplier or customer—something that we find is a great development opportunity.

But for most of us, it might be necessary to shift organisations to get the sort of experience that will provide new ways of looking at problems, the ability to deal well with ambiguity and a different set of tetchy senior executives to deal with.

Increasingly, spending time with a service provider or a consulting organisation can provide great experience in seeing things from 'the other side'. It also helps you to then be a really great client of consulting companies and service providers—demanding but informed— which should be a core capability for all executives today.

Experience in starting up and closing down a service can be character building and usually provides a lot of lessons learned.

A candidate in a recent search had just completed outsourcing a service offshore to the Philippines. She had to oversee the knowledge transfer of over 300 employees to their counterparts in that country. It was hard and she led this as honestly and as openly as she could.

A few years ago, I well remember asking a senior public servant what he believed were his two most significant achievements in the past seven years or so. He responded that the first achievement was shaping and building a new industrial relations policy under one government. His second achievement was dismantling that for the next government of a different political hue—and undertaking both of these in the best way that he could. Both were no doubt character-building and required a considerable amount of resilience.

While you don't need to have embraced all these experiences, it's helpful to reflect and to take some time to consider the breadth and depth of your experience base.

8

PERSONAL AND
PROFESSIONAL GROWTH

Build your resilience

My first year of teaching was like living through a bad reality TV series, except it all happened without any staging. The adage 'you can't make this up' comes to mind. However, it did mean that whatever came after did not faze me too much.

Imagine this as a scenario in an outer suburban Sydney high school: a new co-educational school opened but without any buildings—they were not ready on time.

The 580 or so year 7 and 8 students that made up Outer Suburban High (OSH) were boarded in temporary accommodation across three other schools in the area, including a primary school, for the first five months of the school year. The area was of course, one of Sydney's lowest in socio-economic terms.

There were eight streamed classes at OSH in each of those years (think in terms of Year 7A to 7H, Year 8A to 8H).

Of the twenty-five staff: seventeen were first-year-out teachers, mostly aged twenty to twenty-one. The Principal and Deputy had never held roles at that level before, and they had only been at single-sex boys' schools, having come from tech and trade teaching backgrounds. Of the remaining teachers allocated to the school, most were volunteered by neighboring schools, from those they no longer required, thus, they tended to be an eclectic collection of those who did not quite fit-in anywhere else to date.

The science teachers had no laboratories. The first-year-out teacher-librarian had no resources and of course no library, but had to take sixteen library classes in these temporary classes scattered across the district. As there is a requirement to take twenty-two teaching periods in addition to the six allowed at the time for actually running the library, she also took six music classes, with 7G and 7H.

I was that teacher-librarian and it was a challenging way to start a teaching career.

We did eventually get our classrooms and resource centre midway through the year, but we had no idea what was coming when. Creativity and a positive outlook were in high demand, but not always there. For most of us new teachers there was one of two outcomes: the first was early departure from the teaching profession (in some cases accompanied by a nervous breakdown), and the second was survival and the building of a level of resilience—even if you didn't quite know what you were doing at the time.

Life is about how well you bounce

A key attribute most employers are looking for is a good level of resilience, and of course it is critical if you are leading others in early stage businesses or when a business is in trouble.

Resilience is the ability to persevere and bounce back in the face of challenges. As Vivian Komori has noted, 'Life is not about how fast you run, or how high you climb, but how well you bounce'.

I learned long ago that there are no perfect organisations and no perfect roles. Every organisation has its foibles and challenges. The issue is more how well we bounce, deal with, or recover from these situations.

If you have not been really tested in a role, perhaps with a lousy culture, poor leadership or a difficult business situation, you probably won't have grown at the rate that others might have. You might be surprised at how negative things can get later on in your career, and find it more challenging to deal with.

We often ask candidates and participants about some of their more challenging work-related situations. What they choose to share is fascinating, but of more interest to us, is what they learned from that.

I guess I learned to make do, to share the challenges we had with the students, and to seek whatever assistance I could from other colleagues or schools. I learned that you sometimes just need to take action, as I had colleagues who were becoming unwell and not enough was being done to support us and our students, collectively. I learned the importance of speaking up and making representations up the hierarchy. It was not about being dramatic, but about raising the issue of fairness and not acquiescing in what we were experiencing.

As Christine Kilpatrick, Chief Executive Officer at Melbourne Health has noted, 'It is always the people issues that build your resilience.' In her case it was when her husband died three weeks after she joined the Royal Children's Hospital as Chief Executive in 2008.

If you are not growing then move on

I have had a number of good bosses, and some dodgy ones. The good ones challenged and stretched me. They let me get on with what they wanted me to do but were there for support and to be a good sounding board when needed. The not-so-good ones—in my view at least—were either out of their depth, overly controlling or underestimated what I could do (and treated me accordingly).

I hope I learned from both what works and what doesn't work.

A few months ago, a young friend we will call Louise shared with me her frustrations at work. It was an organisation with over a hundred staff with a CEO who appeared more interested in papering over difficult issues than facing them. Externally he was well regarded. Internally he was slowly strangling a significant part of the business—the part where my young friend worked. No matter what she did, she could not get traction and every day was a struggle to meet client expectations as the funds of those clients were being allocated elsewhere.

In these situations, there are usually a few questions to ask: Are you continuing to learn—in a good way? Do you respect the organisation's leadership? If not, is it likely to change and can you impact that? Is your contribution truly valued? What sort of an impact could you make elsewhere, that is, where the situation is not so fraught?

My friend came to the conclusion that looking around for another role would be timely. She was committed to her client group, but she could not go on trying to do the right thing by them without the funds that had been allocated to them. She applied for a couple of other roles and took one where she was valued. She then thrived, both personally and professionally.

All too often we see that not-so-savvy executives underestimate the choices that good and talented employees have. There is a saying that money and capital goes to where it can be well invested. It is true too that good and talented people will go to where they are appreciated and where they can do well.

Resilience is always put to good uses

In my current role, working with candidates and organisations, I do my best to explain potential new roles as they really are—warts and all.

That usually works out well, as the best candidates really do want a challenge. However, my first two months at Gartner (the first time) represented much more of a challenge than I had realised. But reality came hurtling to greet me in the first two weeks.

The Executive Programs business, a special service for senior clients that I had just been appointed to lead, had started the year before. Most renewals were due in April, a few months away. On about day eight in my new role, I learned that of the twenty-nine clients spread right across Australia, twenty-seven had indicated their intention not to renew. This was quite a shock. What had I done taking this on, and why hadn't anyone explained this to me? After taking time to absorb this, we brainstormed what could be done and it became clear that I needed to visit every one of those clients over the next three weeks.

One client in particular, Frank, was known to be unhappy and he was a considerable influencer with other clients. I knew Frank through my MBS work, so thought he would be sympathetic and a good place to start. In our meeting, I listened hard to him, apologised for what had not been done and suggested some ways I was approaching the role and services. I asked him what it would take to convince him we were serious. I then repeated this with the other twenty-eight Chief Information Officers (CIOs) over the next few weeks. We also quickly organised some workshops that had real content with some good speakers from outside the company and started to address a backlog of research queries.

The result was that, come April, we lost only one client and she impressed upon us that it was a budget issue, not the service. Frank had played his 'influencer' role and asked the doubters to give us another chance. I learned that among my strengths are facing up to the reality of a difficult situation, having the difficult conversations internally and with clients, and then doing what I say I will do.

I could not have done it without a lot of support internally and that required building relationships quickly, including understanding enough about my colleagues to know who could help in areas with which I was quite unfamiliar. But sometimes, the need for resilience goes much deeper.

Kathryn Fagg experienced the need for a different type of resilience when there was a fatality in a business that she led. The impact on her and on the business was profound and emotionally challenging. Staying strong and calm was critical for everyone while focusing on lessons and changes needed. As a result, there was a shift in the company—and the industry—from one where accidents do happen to one where all accidents can be prevented.

9

KEEP GROWING PERSONALLY
AND PROFESSIONALLY

New roles:
you won't meet all the criteria and timing is never right

We have all experienced the challenge of looking at a role and thinking, 'I'd love to have that role, but don't meet all the criteria'.

The good news is even the strong candidates rarely do—if they could do everything in the role description already, where would be the challenge, or the stretch?

Timing is another issue—knowing when to look at shifting roles, when to apply for a promotion, or when to respond positively to a query from a search firm. Often the timing is not right, but then we usually can't control when the interesting roles will be available.

After a little over two years at RMIT, a senior lecturer role became available. It was not directly in the area I had been working in, and I did not receive any particular encouragement internally to apply.

However, I ran into the late Warren Horton, then head of the State Library of Victoria and later National Librarian of Australia. We'd moved from Sydney to Melbourne about the same time and got to know each other through that process.

Warren was far more senior to me in age and career and always had loads of 'gravitas'. He had heard about the position and assumed I was going to apply. I explained to him that I could not meet all the selection criteria.

Warren's response was swift: that this was silliest reason he had ever heard for not applying for such a role, as it was rare that promotional positions in my field became available.

His view was that I should apply, and then do a combination of three things he had done in similar circumstances: first, assume that I could do the role, not the reverse; second, do some quick research and get up to speed enough to get through the selection and interview process; and third, once appointed, subtly change the role to one that suited me better, explaining how much more I could bring to the role than the organisation had envisaged.

I did all of those things and it worked. I got the job, and more or less recreated a significant chunk of it, meaning three years later I was well placed for the next big shift. I have been forever greatful to Warren for his advice.

Don't let your gender determine your faith in your own abilities

In my experience, in many cases men will look at a position, assume they can do it, that they meet the criteria and apply, while most women tend to be far more circumspect—if they don't easily meet all the criteria, they are less likely to apply.

While this situation is changing, we see it regularly in our search work when proactively contacting women we believe should or could be a candidate for a particular role. The response often is 'But I don't understand. What makes you think I could do that?' I don't think I have ever had that response from a male contacted in similar circumstances.

The other aspect of promotions or taking any opportunity to move to another organisation when offered, is the issue of timing.

Timing for me regarding the vacancy for Head of Department at RMIT was really bad. I had just been accepted as a doctoral student and had figured out I might be able to do that and my senior lecturer role. The Head of Department was a different challenge all together.

We frequently hear a potential candidate say, 'But the timing is lousy'. My response is usually along the lines of, 'If we set aside the timing, is this a role in which you are really interested? If it is, let's set aside the timing issue for now, as it is rare that someone will come to you with just the right opportunity when the timing is just right'.

It is just not how things seem to work out. Certainly, sometimes it is absolutely right to decline an opportunity because of timing. But it doesn't mean that when you are ready the right opportunity will just pop along.

If you feel undervalued, speak up

After three or so years at Gartner, I came to the view that I was either underpaid or undervalued.

I was recruiting staff to my team in the US and Europe and no matter how you compared the figures and the cost of living, they were being paid far better than I was. The dollar was plummeting at the time, and though my role was global, my employment contract was in Australian dollars. At the same time, I was getting unsolicited job offers offering much more than Gartner was paying me and some of these were Dean or academic roles!

I had asked my then boss about this a few times, but he was not interested. In the end I mentioned this situation at the highest levels, and to one executive in particular, just by asking him to guess how much he thought my salary was in US dollars.

He was surprised with the number I gave him and promised to do something about it. I explained the other offers I was getting, but that I did not want to move. I just wanted to ensure there was respect and recognition for the considerable contribution I made to the business and at least some of that should be reflected in my remuneration. He agreed and asked me to put it into an email to him. That evening I prepared and sent a well-crafted email of about six paragraphs.

The following morning, he put some figures in front of me on the desk and asked if they were acceptable. It was a thirty-three percent pay rise. While my eyes nearly popped out of my head, I retained my composure and graciously accepted. It was clearly one of the most effective emails I had ever written, based on the result.

I phoned Robert later that day from the airport to give him the news and asked him to guess the size of the rise. I said 'more' several times before finally saying 'yes'. Those in the long queues around me, who had of course heard my end of the conversation, burst into spontaneous applause and shouts of 'go girl' and 'well done'.

It was not easy for me to take this issue on at the time, but I include it as an example of the importance of making the right case and being honest and direct. We know that women tend to find it far harder to ask for a pay rise or the right role and they usually have more reasons to do so and it is great to see that the issue of pay equity is finally being addressed in many organisations.

How to be on the radar for the right role

One of the most frequently asked questions of search firms and recruitment agencies is 'How do I get on your radar?' or 'How do I get noticed?' My semi-facetious response is usually, 'Make sure you have some real achievements and a track record that is worthy of being noticed'.

So, what does matter and how do you get noticed?

From the start it is important to appreciate that only relatively few roles are filled by search firms. Most are filled through internal advertising, via various electronic job boards depending on the country you are in, via LinkedIn, or by invitation through personal networks.

A search firm will generally do considerable research and proactive call outs to both good sources and potential candidates. That is usually not the case in other situations, but the same principles apply in relation to getting noticed in the right way.

The challenge is as much who knows you as who you know.

Your next role is most likely to come about through your network, contacts, reputation or by recommendation.

Top 10 tips for Getting Noticed

1. Create a credible and referenceable track record

Ensure you have a credible and referenceable track record that demonstrates your ability to accept and implement accountability, with and through others. Document your achievements, analyse and understand failures, and write up lessons learned. Be clear about where you have really added value, delivered more than was expected, helped solve an intractable problem, or shaped and implemented an innovative policy, process, product or deliverable.

2. Effectively manage upwards

Always manage upwards in a thoughtful, consistent and considered manner. Part of your role is to help make others successful, particularly those to whom you report. You need to ensure they know what you are doing, that there are no surprises. Let them know of your successes and alert them early to problems. Know their agenda and what they need to do to be successful. And it is always helpful to be across how your boss earns his or her bonus.

3. Effectively manage stakeholders

An important part of your network is your stakeholders, whether they are key clients, community groups, your peers, or the chair of your board committee. Are you providing what they need from you, in a timely and appropriate manner? Do you keep them in the loop sufficiently? They can be some of your best supporters if you are well engaged with them.

4. Know how to articulate your achievements

Ensure you know your own story, that you have captured your

achievements and internalised them. You need to be articulate about your work and accomplishments, in every situation, whether it is in the office, sitting next to someone at a breakfast networking meeting, or when stuck in the elevator with your CEO or Board Chair. (See Chapter 14.)

5. Don't shy away from conflict or ambiguity

Do not shy away from dealing with conflict situations and ambiguity— both can be great sources of energy. Constructively challenging and being challenged should be part of every robust team experience. Understand the differences between content and relational conflict and how your own emotional intelligence attributes will shape your default response. Dealing effectively with conflict and ambiguity is what leaders and managers need to do particularly well.

6. Develop your networking skills

Become a good internal and external networker. Being professionally involved demonstrates your willingness to have new experiences and a focus on curiosity and continued learning. It might also mean you have become accustomed to giving back.

7. Celebrate your team's successes publicly

Celebrate milestones and make sure your team gets the credit they deserve. Your team members are also some of your most positive advocates—and of course they can also be the most negative, so make sure you never take them for granted.

8. Have a reasonable public profile

Accept some workshop, writing/blogging, roundtable or conference-speaking opportunities, making sure of course that you have something of substance to contribute. Those who are constantly on the speaker circuit can lose credibility, but taking some opportunities is likely to mean that you have some achievements and experiences worth sharing. It also requires that you exercise discipline in putting together your thoughts, clarifying those achievements, and working through the best way to convey them to others.

9. Have an awesome CV

Have an informative, concise, achievement-focused CV (which can then form the basis of your LinkedIn Profile). I read a lot of CVs and too often they are too long, meandering, self-indulgent and miss the 'essence' of achievements and capabilities. Four pages should be plenty, with a not miniscule font—just remember that in many instances the person reading it won't have your fabulous eyesight. They might not have heard of one or two of your places of employment, so don't assume they know the company and so provide a one-sentence explanation about what each does. Make sure those four pages include a concise and informative summary of everything relevant on the first page.

10. Optimise your profile on LinkedIn

In many cases a good presence on LinkedIn is useful. It is a key tool for identifying candidates, and companies, government agencies, search firms and recruiters use it extensively. Ditch the photo of you at a wedding or on the ski slopes. Replace it with a good professional one. Ensure your profile is succinct, informative, achievement focused, accurate and not more than a couple of screens.

10

WELL-BEING MATTERS

Look after your physical health

Different things sustain each of us, but most of us work better when we are more physically fit.

It does not mean we have to be slim or emulate the beautiful people set—it just helps us to build a good level of stamina and to feel good about ourselves.

Some time ago I had a conversation on a bar stool with a former colleague. He was clearly exhausted from a lot of travel, had put on weight and was not enjoying it. He told me he did not have time to exercise, to which I replied that my travel schedule was equally onerous and it was just a matter of developing some good habits. (Empathy is not always my strongest attribute.)

About a year later, a person came towards me. I did not recognise him until he started speaking. He told me he had taken up walking early most mornings and felt so much better. He realised I had not recognised him and laughed saying, yes, my unsympathetic reaction a year earlier had started him thinking.

I do know what it is like to be unwell, to struggle to get upstairs, and to sustain the level of activity to which I am accustomed. In my early 30s I had to have a major operation in February one year. Basically, everything that could go wrong did go wrong. I learned about the fragilities of the human body, many of which I had taken for granted.

I can still remember the day in November of that year when I realised that the medical issues had finally run their course. I took a deep breath and from that day determined that I would try to retain this feeling of being well.

I did two things immediately: I went out and bought a new bike so that I could go riding with our kids on the weekend, and I started swimming regularly. I am not a great swimmer, but swimming laps at a nearby indoor pool either at lunchtime (when the kids were younger) or early in the morning before work (now) became a habit, along with doing some serious stretching exercises halfway through. If for some reason I can't swim, I go for a brisk walk.

It is a matter of finding out what works for you—it might be yoga, running, rowing or tennis. If you are a single parent and can't get out so much, get an exercise bike to put in the bedroom or the back room. It's really hard to pretend to have energy when you don't have it.

Exercising while travelling can give special insights

My commitment to swimming while travelling has also given me insights into other cultures. You can learn a lot when exercising with the locals. I have made some observations as a frequent business traveller where you need to adjust to various cultural idiosyncrasies— such as ignoring the road rules (Italy) or tipping adequately (US)— but some of you may be surprised that these idiosyncrasies extend into exercise as well.

Australia

In Australia we are used to swimming in a circular fashion in pools with marked lanes. We maximise the resource—five or six people easily swim in the same lane, and you always keep to the left (like on the roads). The lanes are usually marked slow, medium and fast. I swim in the slow lane at the Melbourne City Baths but can handle the medium lane at my weekend suburban pool. And don't even think about swimming in any lane early in the morning at the Melbourne University pool, where the squad will just swim right over you.

UK

You can always tell an Australian in a hotel pool in the UK. We disturb the water and swim a lot of freestyle. We are not doing gentle, British breaststroke—this takes the form of a peculiar 'head above the water, don't get my hair wet' approach, for women and men. There are usually no lanes roped off, but everybody makes room for everybody else by weaving in and out—a bit like their dedication to, and expectation of, queuing.

Europe

In Italy and Belgium and many other European countries, if you manage to find a hotel with a pool—and one that opens before 8am—you'd better have a bathing cap with you. For some reason it's seen as unclean to have one's hair uncovered. Even if you are bald the rule applies. Several times I have had to pay a few euros for a cap because they just won't let me swim in the pool with my short, clean hair uncovered. It's the rule and no one can remember who decided it, but it is a rule and it can't be broken.

US

US pools are different again. Here there are often lanes and people 'own' them. So, if you get there first, you have a whole lane to yourself for as long as you want it. If the lane is very wide, two people go up and down in their own 'zone', not the in the circular manner of Australians. Others can just wait until you finish as those who got there first have supremacy. At a sports club pool in San Francisco, the smallish pool was divided into seven narrow 'single person' lanes—only one person could fit in each lane anyway.

Do swimming styles really reflect business cultures?

I regularly ponder on what this reveals about the way people work together in organisations. For starters, they seem to reinforce perceptions about cultural norms. As gross generalisations, the English like order, Europeans stress the rules (although no one can remember why they are important anymore), there is a strong thread of individualism in the US, and Australians are easy going—they share and are collegial.

Australians have a deserved reputation for being team oriented, resourceful, and for getting on with the job no matter what. There is less emphasis on the need to take personal credit for what is achieved. As a result, you will find Aussies doing global jobs all over the place for companies not headquartered in Australia. And you'll find them over-represented in hotel or sports club swimming pools, thrashing about rather than sedately floating on top of the surface.

Be mindful of your mental well-being

Some things I have learned over the years help me traverse difficult situations and maintain a reasonable sense of mental well-being.

It is helpful to take time out in stressful situations to rethink the context, to consider: Why is this happening? What is my role in it? And can—or should—I be doing something about it? Is it within my control, or do I have to just deal with the consequences as well as I can?

Something most people learn over the years is to pick their battles and 'not sweat the small stuff'. Really good leaders focus on just a few things. They try to energise people on no more than two or three goals. We can't remember or internalise many more than this. Don't take things personally—clearly separate the issue from the person.

A dedicated staff member I worked with a few years ago tended to take a lot of things personally. There were some members of staff who, under stress and with pressing timelines, became very task oriented (a trait I have been known to exhibit also). She would get quite upset if communications seemed a bit terse or there were decisions made in which she was not included but thought that she should have been consulted on.

Assuming good intent on the part of others helps you to deal with your colleagues. We have all had the experience of a team member sending an email that appeared to be a bit insulting, presumptuous or even undermining.

My advice is to take the time to read it again, and reframe your own context for reading it assuming that they had good intent—and just phrased things in a clumsy way. Often, if we do not have a good view of person, we have already set up a negative mesh around anything they say or do. Ratcheting up my level of impulse control in more recent years has saved me quite a bit heartache and bad karma.

Remember to take real holidays

Taking holidays—and being serious about taking holidays—should become one of your personal survival mechanisms.

Our summer holidays tend to be family holidays, then at other times, as empty nesters, Robert and I will take one or two weeks on our own, though we have also invited and travelled with different grandchildren from time to time. (You will likely have gleaned by now that being guilt-free is entirely consistent with family being hugely important to me.)

In my first years at Gartner, Robert and I took some remote desert trips, usually each year, for two weeks at a time. I well remember mentioning to my American boss that I was going to take two weeks off and he commented that that was fine as he could always reach me by email. This was 1998 and there were few areas where mobile phones worked, let alone Wi-Fi!

When I explained that that would be difficult he suggested I leave the number of the hotels we were staying at. I then had to explain that we would be sleeping in things called swags under the stars.

In the end I gave him our home number and suggested if there were any terrible personal emergencies he could call our home and the kids had an emergency number for us. It was the Royal Flying Doctor Service.

To my astonishment, he did call home and explained he had an emergency but my older-teenage son, who answered the phone, explained to him it was not an emergency, so he would instead pass the message on when we got home.

The good side of this though was that a few others in Gartner then started to take real holidays and not do half a day's work every day they were away with their families. I got a few personal thank yous over the years, including one from a very driven young man who said it had made all the difference to his wife and family.

Sometimes you do have to attend to things while on holidays. But it helps to start out with expectations that you will minimise this. Time out is really important for both your mental well-being as well as your personal relationships.

Take time to nurture your spiritual self

On the spiritual side we each need to find what works for us too.

I was raised a Catholic, though only one grandparent was originally a Catholic and that was on my mother's side. It was a looser form of French-influenced Catholicism from my maternal grandmother, and not the more orthodox Irish-influenced strand usually evident in Australia. My mother was largely self-educated and really got into philosophy as an adult and started to question lots of things. As she and my father aged, though, they became a bit more orthodox in their beliefs.

As a teenager I questioned many of the Church's teachings while still being a regular mass goer. These days, like many Catholics, I have my own informed views, and there are some significant tangents from what passes for official teachings. Just think of most of the big issues that get in the press and my views diverge. However, my views make sense to me and I am very comfortable with them—as are many of those who continue to identify as Catholics.

My Jewish friends readily take time out from their working lives to attend to family and religious matters, at Passover and Atonement in particular.

When Robert and I travelled throughout remote Australian desert locations, with the redoubtable Andrew Dwyer from Diamantina Touring, we spent days where we might have seen just a few other people travelling desert tracks, and sometimes on no tracks at all. I found the stillness, the red earth, and great expanses, uplifting.

We met and spent evenings with Indigenous communities which opened up other ways of looking around us and valuing what we were experiencing. They guided us through their country and we got a glimpse of those other ways of seeing the hills, the streams and valleys.

Think about what renews you. If you can, take yourself out of your current way of doing things, and experience other lenses. Those other ways can help you to really gain, or regain, your sense of perspective.

11

SEEK AND VALUE MULTIPLE INSIGHTS

Working with youth creates different forms of leadership

Throughout most of my time at MBS and half my time at Gartner I was, concurrently, experiencing a different form of leading—working with young people.

Each of our four children as teenagers became involved in the Antioch Movement—ministry by youth, for youth.

At the time, the movement was a fabulous development as it gave young people (aged about sixteen to twenty-two) a forum to share stories, explore their beliefs and try to make sense of things around them in a supportive environment.

Our first experience was the second retreat weekend. Our eldest son David invited us to a talk he was delivering to the group. He had come to the considered view that he was quite like his father, which neither of them realised at that time. This, as you can imagine, had its good and bad points for each of them. It was very moving for us as parents and opened up a new level of relationship between us, and particularly Robert and David.

After a few years, we were asked if we would become one of the couples providing support to the group, and those ten years with the youth group became an important part of my growth. One time, around exams, none of the group had time to prepare a talk, so Robert and I were asked could we please prepare a joint talk about our relationship. This of course was quite a challenge as we are not the type to dwell on these things too much—we just like to make it work as well as we can.

We called the talk 'We are one, but we are not the same' after the U2 song of that title. I prepared a draft, which Robert then added to. We found, of course, that we had quite different recollections of the same events, and I guess that was part of the message to the kids.

My learnings from working with the group were profound. I learned that no matter how things appear on the surface, every family has tensions.

I learned, too, that no matter how tough or gruff a member of the group or a visitor seemed to be, there was almost certainly an insecure person in there trying to figure out the world around them and find their place in it.

Finally, it helped me to hone my listening skills and my ability to get things done without appearing to influence anything. That is because the challenge for the adults (or anyone over twenty-five) at Antioch meetings and events is that it really needs to be the youth leading, so you have to figure out how to get things done without appearing to influence anything.

Know and grow your emotional intelligence

Have you ever had a boss or colleague who just did not seem attuned to what was happening around them? Perhaps you've experienced a colleague that just did not pick up on the cues that others were giving, or some peers who did not understand or appreciate their impact on others. Maybe you know many really smart people, who appear to have high IQs, but might not be very effective communicators or contribute as much as others. In these situations, it is likely that the individuals concerned have a few gaps in their emotional intelligence (EI).

In our work with individuals and executive teams, we use a well-recognised EI assessment approach and tool. This can provide a rich source of feedback, as it is a set of attributes you can actually work on and improve.

But what is emotional intelligence? Why does it matter? How do you assess it? Why it is useful to understand your EI? What can you do about?

Emotional intelligence is a set of emotional and social skills that develop over time and influence your behaviour. Understanding your EI provides a great lens into your, and your co-workers, behaviours, including: the way you perceive and express yourself, the way you develop and maintain social relationships, and the way you cope with challenges. It is also about how you use emotional information. A good emotional quotient really helps makes things easier for you, both at home and at work. Those with greater emotional intelligence are generally easier to work and reason with, meaning when an individual has both high IQ and high EI they are more likely to have the potential for senior leadership. For those wanting to take that step up, having an understanding of EI is critical.

So, drawing on the approach of the MHS group, what are the specific attributes that comprise EI? (See further reading.)

1. Self-perception

Self-perception encompasses understanding your own emotions through your self-awareness, your self-regard (confidence), and your self-actualisation (self-development). Understanding and valuing yourself is usually part of the fabric of good leaders.

2. Self-expression

Self-expression includes assertiveness, independence and emotional expression. Assertiveness is about how you stand up for yourself, but in a respectful way. Independence is about initiative. Emotional expression is about how you present your feelings to others.

A good level of initiative is critical for leaders. However, a combination of very high assertiveness and independence might make it harder for a person to be a real team player, as they might not consider the views of others to the extent that they should.

A reasonable level of emotional expression is also critical for leaders because it helps us to appear more authentic. If you have been brought up not to show your feelings or be demonstrative, your appearance will show little variation. This can negatively impact how you lead others. If you have too much, you might present to others with too much by way of extremes. That is where your self-awareness comes in—to judge when and how to show and use your emotions effectively.

3. Interpersonal

Interpersonal includes interpersonal relationships, empathy and social responsibility. Skills in interpersonal relationships provide the foundation of building and sustaining relationships. Empathy is being able to recognise, understand and appreciate how other people feel. It is about being able to articulate an understanding of another's perspective and behaving in a way that respects the feelings of others. Social responsibility involves acting responsibly, having a social consciousness and showing concern. A well-developed social conscience is often an indicator of the ability to collaborate well with others.

4. Decision Making

Decision making includes problem solving, reality testing and impulse control. The problem solving attribute can be a bit misleading as individuals often believe they are good problem solvers. In EI terms though, it is about effectively managing your emotions when solving problems—for example, separating out the personal and professional (and also articulating that to others that that is what you are doing).

Reality testing is about checking that you see things as they really are. We all know people who, we might say, have a poor grip on reality. That is, they might leave a meeting thinking things went well, but they were really a bit delusional about that. For those people, checking that what they experienced is what others also experienced is a very useful and simple technique.

Regarding impulse control, some of us tend to react to a situation more quickly than we need to or should. Think of the time you might have replied in haste to an email, or were too quick to assume bad intent and comment on potentially negative behaviours of others without fully understanding their situation or the circumstances. You might know people you would describe as 'considered', who think things through before reacting. They are likely to have a higher level of impulse control than some of their peers.

5. Stress Management

Stress management includes flexibility, stress tolerance and optimism. Flexibility is about how effectively you adapt to change, and can provide some pointers as to how well you deal with ambiguity and uncertainty. Stress tolerance is about how successfully you cope with stressful situations. Optimism is about having a positive outlook and is usually an important ingredient of effective leadership. Each of us appreciates experiencing a sense of hope, and to see our leaders optimistic.

As mentioned above, understanding the different elements of your EI and your natural tendencies means you can further understand your strengths and some areas for development or more conscious self-leadership.

For example, if you have a high level of stress tolerance with concurrent low empathy it is likely to mean that you can deal with difficult situations, but you might not understand why others cannot do the same. If that is also matched with lower impulse control your behaviour at times might look like badgering to others, and in the worst instances, bullying. You are likely to sound off at why others can't deal with things the way you can.

On the other hand, where you have a combination of lower assertiveness and higher empathy, you might be tempted to yield in any difficult negotiation. You might empathise too much with those with whom you are negotiating and be not so good at standing up for yourself, your viewpoint, or your part of the organisation.

In my work, we use an understanding of EI to help establish the need for targeted individual, and then team, development. The feedback and advice can be challenging, but it also provides some good indicators of those who are keen to work on their development and contribution. We have seen it lead to significant increases in personal performance and in interactions with, and impacting on, others—all of which enhance an individual's leadership attributes and ongoing potential.

We worked with a group of twenty very senior Project Directors, who were each leading part of a major business systems implementation (in the range of $400m+ over three years). On average, as a group they had a high level of assertiveness with low levels of empathy. They wanted to just get it done, but had to bring others along with them, including members of the executive team.

Just sharing with each of them their individual EI scores, and then the aggregate, as a group had a profound impact on their understanding of why they were encountering resistance. In working with their external consulting integration partner they wanted to win every encounter and negotiation, rather than really understand what their partner's issues and pressures were.

Thus, knowing the strengths, weaknesses and typical behaviours of yourself and your colleagues leads to a more productive and efficient workplace.

12

BE MINDFUL OF YOUR IMPACT
ON OTHERS

You are always marketing yourself

We are always marketing ourselves in how we present to others, whether we like that idea or not. How we behave every day is how others see us. We can't just turn our behaviour on and off.

That statement, that you are always marketing yourself, or being judged by others, sometimes takes people back a little. As a client noted to me recently, 'Some of our managers just don't realise that they are always being watched. Their behaviour then becomes some sort of acceptable bar for others'.

It seems some of us think we can turn our charm on and off, and that we will be able to articulate a situation or form a relationship on an as needs basis. Our behaviour every day is what people see and take note of, not just when we decide that we need a colleague or business partner's help, so it is time to start forming a good relationship with them.

A couple of months ago I was working with some senior managers on track for executive roles. They were a well-committed group and their organisation had put some effort into their development over the years. But there was one person I had reservations about and initially I could not quite figure out why.

It was something about how he formed relationships. I used the word expedient as a way to describe his relationship-building, as it was very much on an as needs basis: that is, I need, therefore I will start to build that relationship.

When I shared my view with him, concerned, he reflected on it for a while then thought that was probably a reasonable description. He came to realise that, long-term, it would not serve him well.

People have long memories in business

In my second period with Gartner, a local sales team asked me if I would join them on a visit to a particularly difficult executive we will call Nathan.

I warned my colleagues that I did have some reservations about the value of the visit, as I had had previous encounters with him, but he agreed to meet with us.

At the meeting, Nathan explained in the first few minutes that he really didn't need our services, as he got all the information he needed from vendors. Vendors were very generous and he didn't have to pay them for their advice. It was one of those situations where I thought, why did this person agree to a meeting—did he enjoy insulting people, wasting their time or purporting to be extra smart?

I closed off the meeting quite quickly, as prolonging it just played to his misguided ego.

When he was exited from that company about two years later I had moved into the executive search business. He was then very keen to meet with me and assumed I would do everything I could to secure him a role.

It was a misguided assumption: his relationship-building skills were poor and he had a significant deficit in what I refer to as the graciousness gene.

It is difficult to advocate for someone who does not grasp the foundations of good relationship-building, or just civility and respectfulness. Our clients expect those attributes in their executive team members and always, rightly, express the importance of good behaviours—all the time.

Our administrative staff today, who receive candidates and potential candidates in our office, and deal with them on the phone, tend to provide quick but generally spot-on insights into aspects of people's behaviours. I regularly ask them if they have any input about particular candidates, based on their interactions, and they generally do—both positive and negative.

In the following sections, I share learnings from some of my own behaviours, the good, the bad and the mediocre.

Be thoughtful about how others might receive your requests

What other people think of us is not just driven by face-to-face communication. It is a combination of many forms of engagement.

Several weeks into my first Gartner role, my US-based boss, Terry Waters, came to Australia to help induct me and to see how things were going.

At the time Gartner had few local researchers, so much of our research analyst support was based in the US.

Clients logged requests for phone consultations in specialist areas, but we were getting negative feedback about how this was working. Services were promised and not delivered, analysts were not on the line when they were supposed to be, and local clients just didn't get any priority.

The result of this was that I built a bit of a reputation—internally— for complaining about our service levels provided by the US analysts.

It was also the early days of email, and although Gartner has always had quite an email-oriented culture, it wasn't working as it should have and I had not learned the lesson quickly enough about tempering the tone of emails. It also took me a while to realise that most Americans are unfailingly polite and prefer to speak in euphemisms rather than come to the point quickly as Australians generally do.

Terry explained some of this to me, but I didn't get it at first. He wanted me to come to a Gartner US CIO event in March in Amelia Island, Florida and do a keynote presentation. That sounded like a great idea. Could I come via Stamford (Headquarters) and meet a few more people? Another great idea as Stamford was forty-five minutes on a fast train from New York city and I had close friends in that city anyway.

He escorted me around the Stamford Headquarters some weeks later, and I met the executives I had not met as part of the selection process, and renewed acquaintances with others.

It was all going very well I thought. Then as we were leaving one office, I overheard one executive quietly say to Terry, 'Oh, well, she seems much nicer than we thought she was'.

My email-influenced reputation had preceded me, and it was quite a lesson. I quickly learned to put emails written in haste into my drafts folder and come back to them the next morning. Quite a few were then deleted. Others were appropriately modified.

Be creative when you must manage upwards

It can be challenging but not impossible to manage upwards well. Creativity often helps.

While I was leading the business in Australia and New Zealand, we acquired a UK-based business that had clients in Hong Kong and Singapore. My role then became much more an Asia-Pacific role than an ANZ one, and I was badly in need of more resources.

At that time, I was doing more than one role as I was also co-leading the global CIO research for Gartner. We produced a monthly report globally, but really did not have the specialised resources that underpinned this.

A few months into the role I realised that in February our clients were receiving the report from about July of the previous year. We were more than six months behind. This spurred a writing frenzy where we revised the work that Peter Weill and I had completed through the

Business School (with the appropriate acknowledgement of course) into a very accessible form. We caught up by about November and then kept on track every month after that.

Gaining support for additional resources when you are based a long way from HQ, where decisions are made, can be fraught. I was in Stamford every few months as part of the global team, but could not get traction on an extra team member to work with clients in the region.

When we grew to about sixty—with just me and an assistant—I resolved that I had to take this on as a serious project.

In the US, a Program Director has thirty to thirty-five clients as well as a much larger number of analysts to support events and other commitments. But they also covered a much smaller geographic area, and I realised that very few people in Stamford had any idea of what it was like servicing clients face-to-face in Brisbane, Perth, Sydney, Melbourne, Auckland, Wellington and Canberra, as well as several regional locations in the state of NSW.

For the next visit to Stamford I prepared a series of maps on successive PowerPoints, comparing the land mass of Australia to that of the continental US. Australia is actually larger and I had the location and number of clients on the Australian map, as well as the concentration of clients in the US.

Let's just say that persistence and the comparative geography lesson worked and we finally got the approval for an additional Director from January the following year.

Again, the solution was trying to figure out where the blockage was and what type of evidence was needed in order to address that.

Be honest about your situation respectfully and do this in the meeting

Through this time, we continued to grow our client base, but if we were to sustain services globally we needed a full-time and focused CIO research and services team.

I was interested in developing other parts of the business, but in the early days I seemed to have a different boss about every four or five months. One day, as I prepared to head to a series of internal, then client, meetings in the US, I saw a generic email explaining my boss had changed again. I then heard that my new boss thought it was fine for me to continue both the Asia-Pacific leadership role and, concurrently, lead a new global CIO research and services team.

For various reasons, both of these were a full-time job and I was not happy. But I did not know how I was going to communicate this to yet another boss. I was handed an opportunity at an internal meeting, where I had to decide on the spot as to whether and how I would use it. My new boss decided to start our global team meeting by asking how we were all feeling. Clearly, he expected us to be feeling fabulous, especially as he was now leading the team. He asked me first, so I stated how disappointed I was at being asked to do two full-time jobs. I said I had a deep commitment to clients and the company but that I felt that I was being taken advantage of, that I doubted they would ask others (including my male colleagues) to do these roles concurrently.

I decided to be completely honest. That Australian directness meant that when I finished, there was complete silence for a while, and a few intakes of breath. Then there was an acknowledgment that there were clearly further things we needed to discuss. We did that over the next forty-eight hours alongside the major client meetings in progress.

After that I was offered the global research and services role—on its own, without the APAC role—and I accepted.

The key to this shift in expectations was responding honestly to that question about how I was feeling.

Careful bluntness is a good thing

I am a firm believer in discussing things in the meeting. I never cease to be amazed by people who mutter about things, but then don't take up the opportunity to openly discuss issues when given the chance.

As you might guess I have a low tolerance for what is called passive-aggressive behaviour and believe it is always important to call things out. While I do have to acknowledge that my directness has been a mixed blessing, my colleagues and I were quite touched when one of our NGS Global clients thanked us at the end of an engagement in front of the thirty or so people who had been part of the Capability and Development work we do.

He thanked us for providing the individuals, and team as a whole for what he termed 'careful bluntness' about their performance and development needs. We thought it was a great way to describe a significant part of what we do.

13

KNOW YOUR BUSINESS.
VALUE THOSE AROUND YOU

Take the time and get the resources to really understand the numbers

In the Executive Programs team at Gartner we continued to grow the business quite rapidly and we had clearly hit a sweet spot in the market.

Gartner had lost quite a few staff to the shiny dot com boom and staffing was a challenge at times. Our part of the business went through the dot com bust and our growth path continued.

Our success had a number of factors: we renewed our portfolio of services, integrated the resources from acquisitions, worked hard at our value proposition and really started to understand our numbers.

One of my big learnings at this time is the importance of the finance staff working with you. Our group had recruited an external financial team member who became integral. Together we did a lot of analytics on our services: what worked, what mattered to some and not to others, and what were the predictors of a delighted client and, thus, a renewal.

Two figures we identified had a profound impact on our future business. The first was that the best predictor of a renewal and higher client satisfaction was the amount of attention or 'touch points' we had with a client in their first month of service.

This is definitely not rocket science but then again, most business basics aren't. It gave us strong evidence about how we should service our clients.

The second figure was the multiplier effect. If a Gartner account (say a corporate client) had a CIO Executive Programs membership, then, on average, they would bring in more than two-and-a-half-times as much revenue to Gartner as those that were not Executive Program members.

We had believed this for some time and had been using it as a basis for further investment, which we badly needed. We were providing our core services to an ever-increasing client base with the same core service numbers.

The senior leadership team then realised our team was something of a crown jewel. They started giving us much more attention, and in time, better staffing.

Becoming 'noticed' as a business has consequences

Part of this process of being noticed had other implications and, through these, I learned that it is really important to give people a go.

A group of us had been running the business globally as something of a collaborative foursome (three regional heads and me). Then, at the European Symposium in Cannes, I was asked to meet a person called Robin. About two minutes before meeting her I asked the executive taking me to the room, 'Am I right in thinking that she is to be my new boss?' He fudged a bit but then said, 'Yes'. I was not happy.

I had a few reasons for being annoyed. Here was another layer of management being put in place, the person concerned had limited experience of working with CIOs and we thought we were doing just fine. We would have been quite happy if any one of us was made the person in charge, but not an outsider who did not know the business and had not worked with the most senior of our clients.

I did not deal with news about this new young boss very well at all at first. These days, whenever I hear of someone being passed over or a new boss coming in who looks like a poor fit, I always encourage people to give them a chance. Something I found difficult when in the situation myself.

However, we quickly came to see the value in Robin's appointment, and she was remarkably gracious with this tetchy post 40- and 50-year-old group she now had reporting to her.

I am not particularly proud of my first meeting with Robin Kranich, but felt that my anger was justified at the time. Robin explained that she understood that the team was now going to report to her. I explained that I thought this was inappropriate for a number of reasons. I had kids who were nearly her age and a daughter-in-law who was quite a bit older than she was. She then went on to say that her role was to help make our team and business even more successful. None of our team was based at HQ in Stamford and she was. Her job was to make things easier for us.

I wasn't buying it at the time. She indicated that she expected the benefit of the doubt—interestingly she didn't ask, just indicated that she knew we were all adults and successful business people and she expected to be given a chance. I recall telling her I would try, but it would not be easy.

Robin Kranich was clearly a good listener, very resilient, knew herself well and was comfortable with that. We started off on the rockiest of terms and I left the room still perplexed and somewhat angry.

A sign of rapid mutual respect came the morning of my first day of vacation six weeks later on 24 December. I opened an email I should have left closed.

It indicated my new expense budget for the team, and our services were missing a significant number. There had been a pruning of budgets. I had always come in right on line and was good at predicting what we really needed. I rang Robin to share this with her, to explain we would struggle to make this work, and why that was so. She said if that was the case she would make sure the original figures were reinstated and to turn off the computer and go have my holiday.

I knew that she would do as she said. When I got off the phone, I reflected that we had come a long way in just six weeks. I had come to realise that Robin was a person of good intent and great integrity. She was a clear communicator who always followed through, she knew what she didn't know and was respectful and keen to learn. I now completely trusted her word—and when I got back from vacation the funds were back in my budget.

Am I working with people I want to go to dinner with?

My usual barometer of team relationships is 'Are these people I want to go to dinner with?' Usually it's a resounding yes.

About a month after I got back from my vacation, I was back in the US for both internal and client meetings, then going to Canada. Robin asked if she could join me on some workshops and visits I was doing with clients in Canada, to Ottawa, Toronto and Vancouver. The answer, of course, was yes. For Robin, it was a crash course in understanding how we did our work. Our relationship was cemented during that time together.

In providing some input to this book I asked a number of women about how they build resilience. Robin was one of those and she cited this experience. This is her side of that story:

> I took over a high growth business that had been run independently and autonomously and successfully. The leaders of each business unit were far more experienced and saw little value in my leadership other than being another layer between them and the President. It took me some time to build trust relationships and to be able to identify areas where I could add value and build a cohesive team. It wasn't easy. It was humbling and tenacious work but we built a much stronger business with a scalable infrastructure.

The impact of Robin on the team was remarkable in more than just the business sense. We were an almost all-female leadership team. We had a high level of mutual trust and could have very robust, honest and direct discussions. We had strong disagreements in the room, agreed on a course of action and that was that.

We also gave each other a fair degree of latitude. We were different individuals, but able to work well together. We understood each other's foibles and eccentricities, though I think the rest of the team thought I had more of those than they did.

Robin and I developed what we called a 'mutual mentoring' relationship, based on strong trust and complementary experiences and skill sets, and we continue to be friends to this day. I know that her ability to deal with my less-than-gracious behaviour at our first meeting, and to be mindful of her own, made all the difference.

We also quickly learned that, now that we had been truly discovered as the jewel in the business' crown, even more was expected of us. We were no longer somewhat under the radar.

14

KNOW YOUR OWN STORY.
CLAIM YOUR ACHIEVEMENTS

Be careful of what you wish for:
greater visibility equals greater vulnerability

If your role means you have a public face, you might have the visibility and status you have craved. You also have a high level of vulnerability.

Who would want to be a politician today, with an open and free press that includes trolls, gossip and virtually no private life allowed? Who would want to be the head of a public sector agency out of favour with the policy of an opposition or alternate party? Who would want to be a CEO in a publicly listed company, or a non-executive Board Director of a controversial business?

Reading Hillary Clinton's *Hard Choices* (2014) before she became a Presidential candidate indicated she had been 'inured'. Devotees of *The Good Wife* will know what 'inured' means (and for those who don't it means you become toughened or hardened). Perhaps there was nothing more to which she could be subjected that hadn't already happened. But she discovered there was, and then not winning the election became another chasm to bridge and to at least rationalise personally and professionally.

The same thing is true of having lived through Julia Gillard's Prime Ministership in Australia. I recall seeing a comedy/satirical show playing a quiz game, which put up a series of foul quotes. The quiz question to the comedians and celebrity guests was, 'Were these lines from a radio shock jock about Prime Minister Gillard or from the lines of television show about a women's prison?'

Most of them were the former and this was shocking. We knew it was happening, but to see so many of these quotes in a twenty-minute block was a real jolt.

No matter what view one has of individuals and their performance, no leader in public life should have been subjected to that, especially not a Prime Minister.

So, when you see those high-profile males and females and you might think you want to be their shoes, think carefully. The risk-return equations might not be what they seem.

Know and be able to articulate your own story

Each of us has a story that we need to be able to share with others—with clarity and in context, claiming our achievements appropriately, demonstrating a good level of pride, but without hubris.

When others ask you 'What do you do?' do you make a clear statement that has meaning to the questioner, or do you mumble something and be a bit self-deprecating? For example: 'I am just a...' Do you respond enthusiastically about your work, your contribution, and how you are contributing to the success of your organisation, or does your response betray a level of negativity and cynicism?

Working with many individuals in either executive search or organisational capability and development engagements, we often start a session with some general queries, which gives the individual an opportunity to share their background with us.

What they choose to share—and not share—and how they do that, usually provides interesting insights. Too many people, particularly women and perhaps about twenty percent of men, struggle to share their story or their narrative well. The men who struggle this way I tend to refer to as 'gentle men' and they are the ones who don't exhibit the assumptions and bravado, or sense of entitlement, of others of their gender.

We each must be able to explain in a lucid way what we have achieved—both in written and oral forms—and be able to maintain a challenging discussion about that. It often takes reflection and gaining clarity first in our own mind. Then it takes practice.

This is not about being manipulative. It is about having the nous to understand what someone else needs to know about you. It is about others managing their risk in relation to your role, or perhaps your appointment to their organisation. It is just good preparation.

I have coached many, otherwise very good, candidates on the key elements of their own story, as they don't know how to describe what they do or think that their CV speaks for itself (it never does). Think about how you explain your achievements to others.

Your colleagues often know your achievements better than you

Many high achievers struggle to recognise what it is that they have done that can be classified as a major achievement.

About three years ago I was working with a group of women as part of an organisation's effort to develop and retain good female talent. Most had engineering or infrastructure backgrounds, and all had been in the organisation for three years or more.

At the end of the first workshop, I asked each of the fifteen participants to share one key work-related achievement they had experienced over the past three years. About half grasped the opportunity, some struggled and two indicated that they really had not achieved anything of note.

Yet other members of the group saw both these two women as high achievers, so fortunately, those members stepped in and were able to quickly articulate what they knew had been achieved.

The two women were surprised by what others considered

achievements. Somehow, they had inflated expectations for themselves and thought they just did not measure up.

Needless to say, we spent some time over the next weeks providing opportunities for participants to practise sharing their stories, getting them used to the fact that this is just a normal expectation of people working at their level.

Early in my time working for Gartner, I was reproached for not sharing some great client feedback that I had received. My boss was of the view that if any one of us did particularly well it reflected on all of us, so it was my duty to share this feedback. We kept a compliments file and those real but de-identified quotes were used in our marketing.

In my current organisation, we encourage all our team members to share great messages we get from our clients or candidates, even if it is just about how welcomed they felt when at our offices. And yes, we also share any negative feedback and support each other through that.

We need to be open and honest about our achievements, and make sure we are clear about our specific roles in any major program.

We have been involved in succession planning and talent management over four or more years, for a number of organisations. When people in these organisations claim to have landed (delivered) a particular project, we can query them and get them to clarify exactly which part they landed and when—as we can share with them others that might have claimed that achievement also! Use every opportunity presented to you.

Practice, practice, practice, then nail it!

In working with the group of women mentioned earlier, we also had them develop a good 'elevator pitch'.

A couple of them already had these skills well-honed. They knew how to make the best of each opportunity. One lunchtime, several of us got into a crowded elevator and one of the women didn't miss a beat. She saw in the corner the executive she had been trying to connect with for a day or so. Over the noise and heads of others she quickly gave him a rundown on the project she was leading and asked him a couple of quick questions. Obviously none of this was confidential, and it was very impressive.

The executive quickly replied, as he would have had a lot of witnesses if he tried to be evasive. It was a masterful demonstration of using every opportunity you have to advantage.

So, think about how well you can articulate and share your story—as a professional, a team leader, manager or executive. It does matter.

15

MAKE AN AWESOME IMPRESSION

First things first: Don't skip your background preparation

This chapter assumes you are shortlisted for a role and you are meeting with relevant individuals from the client organisation. In this instance you might be interviewed by a panel of people, at the one time, and then possibly one on one sessions after that.

Selection teams or panels also want to know that you have done your homework. This is both respectful and goes directly to confirming your motivation and potential relevance.

Preparation is critically important. Make sure that you:

- Have looked up the bios of everyone who might be interviewing you.

- Know about the CEO and Board members, who they are and what their issues might be.

- Have read the latest annual report and other available documentation.

- Are familiar with what has been in the news about the organisation and its competitors, and any publicly available information about their major clients, suppliers etc.

- Have a good grasp of their numbers (if publicly available) and their business and financial dynamics.

- Have tapped anyone relevant you know who could have some good information about the organisation.

- If there is information that has not been available to you such as organisation charts, financial information etc. you should feel free to ask for them before the Candidate Interview. Sometimes a company will want you to sign an NDA (Non-Disclosure Agreement) and that is fine.

What most clients are seeking

Good candidate interviews are behavioural event interviews. That is, the questioners want to know what you have done previously that demonstrates you could do this role well, and that you are not too much of a risk for them. They don't necessarily want to know what you think about a whole lot of things.

All the way through they are thinking about how you present, your body language, how you engage proactively with the interviewers, and the extent to which they think you are authentic, that is, being who you really are (and that you are comfortable with yourself). They want to see someone who is self-confident yet a bit humble, and who is self-aware, but not self-absorbed.

They are assessing whether this is the right role for you as well as whether you are right for them.

Personal chemistry and perceived cultural fit are also important. They don't necessarily want a cultural clone, but they do often want someone who can respect their culture, while also being a change agent—respectful but also a catalyst for change.

Sample questions: prepare for these

Most candidate interviews cover a range of areas. Below are some examples. It is really helpful if you are able to have at least one meaningful example for each of these areas (after the motivation question). Don't be afraid to use the same organisation/role in different responses if talking about a different aspect of the role, for example your delivery response and your people leadership.

Motivation

What is your interest in the role at this time? Share with us just one or two key attributes you would bring to the role.

Delivering results

This role is about transforming xxx. Critical to the success of this role are the concurrent accountabilities to promote and model innovation and deliver savings to xxx. We are keen for you to share with us, where and how you have been able to do that previously and how you did it? Were there issues around priorities, how did you address these and what were the outcomes?

Follow up: If you were implementing this type of initiative again, what would you do differently? What did you learn from the process?

Strategic Thinking

Where have you had the most impact on an organisation through your ability to think and act strategically? Follow up: What was the hardest part of this?

Complexity, Scale and Scope

We are interested in your experience of scale and scope in xxx management. What has been the largest or most complex set of xxx that you have led, and what was it that made it complex?

Stakeholder Engagement / Relationships

This is a key reform and stakeholder engagement role requiring vision, strategic acumen and relationship building. This role needs to lead xxx through strategic stakeholder relationships inside and outside the company. Can you share with us examples of when you have faced challenging situations where you had to manage the expectations of stakeholders and ensure the highest level of support, both internally and externally? How did you do that?

People Management

This role has to build and lead a positive, diverse and productive workforce that aligns with the emerging operating model. Please share with us a time you have led a group through significant change and built a culture of which you are proud. What did you take the group from–to and how did you do this? Follow up: What was the hardest part of the journey and what were your learnings?

Decision Making

What is one of the most difficult work-related decisions you have had to make where, for example, there might have been serious consequences, or it was controversial or emotionally charged?

Self-Awareness

Based on your track record and our interest in what you have achieved, you have some strong capabilities and experience. But we all have our weaknesses. Share with us areas that are not real strengths for you, or examples of behaviours that those around you would like to see more or less of?

Resilience

This role will require great resilience. Where have you failed at some stage, or perhaps not lived up to your own expectations? How did you recover from that?

Other possibility: What is the most challenging criticism you have received and how did you deal with it?

Transition into the Role
(a reality check to see if you really understand the role)

We know that this role will have different opportunities and challenges to your previous roles. Where do you think the most significant challenge or transition will be for you? Which parts of the role do you think will be easier and which harder?

Don't forget

- Treat the interview as a completely new opportunity to position yourself for the role.

- Go around and shake each person's hand when you come into the room.

- Assume the interviewers have read your CV but they won't remember everything in it. It is your job to draw the good stuff out of it.

- Don't say 'If you have read my CV', or, 'As you might have seen in my CV'. It implies the interviewers have not done their homework. Rather, the interview is the opportunity to bring life to your CV and for the interviewers to see who you really are as a person.

- It is okay to bring in notes, just ask first if you can refer to them.

- It is usually NOT a good idea to bring lots of report samples or work that you want to impress on the interviewers. This might be okay at a junior technical level, but it is not what an executive interview is about. You need to demonstrate that you don't need these types of props.

- When asked 'Do you have any questions of us?' it is usual to ask about the process after this session if they have not explained this to you. You can also take the opportunity to summarise your relevance to and interest in the role. You might have a question such as the one below.

- 'If I was successful in gaining this role, what would success look like in 12 months?' You should also be ready for this question yourself as sometimes interviewers ask this instead of the 'Transition' question above. But is a good one to ask.

- Don't force the issue of questions. Sometimes a good response is, 'If I am successful in going to the next stage, then yes there are a number of more detailed questions that I would have'.

- Go around and shake each person's hand before you leave the room. Again, this demonstrates your level of confidence and ease with the interviewers.

- Keep in mind that the client (and search firm if one is involved) is keen to find some great candidates and everyone wants you to do well. You got this far because they thought you were potentially appointable and would do a great job in the role. Assume everyone is on your side, not seeking to be adversarial, but really wanting you to demonstrate some strong and relevant capabilities, experience and personal attributes.

LEARNINGS AND REFLECTIONS: PART 1

Before moving to consider how we lead others, below is a series of learnings about leading ourselves with purpose and then some questions for further reflection.

Learnings about leading yourself with Purpose

- Careers grow through tacking, using the tiller, and sometimes trimming the sails—choices are made based on the circumstances at the time.

- You need to find your WHY, your sense of purpose. This helps to understand your comfort level with your career and personal choices and options, and the trade-offs you are prepared to make.

- Solve the technical issues through that age-old approach of looking at who has done something like this before—don't re-invent. Re-use, rejig and redeploy.

- Outsource what you don't have to do, both at home and in your research. If you have the chance to work on a major turnaround, start a new business, or lead a risky project, take it! These opportunities don't come up very often. No matter how it turns out, you will learn a huge amount along the way.

- Our comfort level with our career and personal choices and options often comes down to the trade-offs we are prepared to make.

- It's helpful to take the longer view on your career, and sometimes to 'hasten slowly' and stay where you are for a while, if it suits your current circumstances.

- Where there are babies and children involved, learn to embrace the ensuing chaos.

- You don't have to do it all. It's about picking your spots and knowing that perfect is the enemy of good. ive yourself permission to lower some standards so you can preserve emotional capital is a gift.

- Be willing to talk about what you are doing with others, to share some of the challenges, as you never know what might eventuate.

- You can get information about your strengths, limitations and development needs from reflecting on what has, and has not, worked for you previously.

- Avoid getting so caught up and pleased to be doing the work you are doing, that you forget to have the perspective on the remuneration you should have.

- Think about how well you are able to articulate and share your story—as a professional, a team leader, manager or executive. It does matter.

- Use every opportunity presented to you.

- Different things sustain each of us, but most of us work better when we are more physically fit.

- Don't take things personally—clearly separate the issue from the person.

- Taking holidays, and being serious about taking holidays, should become one of your personal survival mechanisms.

- Think about what renews you. If you can, take yourself out of your current way of doing things, and experience other lenses. Those other ways can help you to really gain, or regain, your sense of perspective.

- Emotional Intelligence is a set of emotional and social skills that influence our behaviour. It provides a great lens into our behaviours.

- Understanding the different elements of your EI and your natural tendencies means you can further understand your strengths and some areas for development or more conscious self-leadership.

Reflections

- Where do you get real satisfaction?

- What type of growth do you want?

- Where did you take a career risk and how did it turn out?

- What is your WHY? What is it that makes you want to leap out of bed and take on the world?

- Have you recently sought feedback on your own skill set, from your boss, your colleagues, those you lead, your clients, your stakeholders and through thoughtful discussions with friends and family?

- How diverse has your career been to date? Have you had the opportunity to go into new or different areas in your organisation, or in another organisation? What did you learn from that? How has it informed the way you look at situations? To what extent do you have multiple lenses to look at problems, or different types of experiences to provide you with a broader context for action?

- What are your real strengths?

- What exercise routine works for you?

- Think of your last stressful situation. Why did this happen? What was your role in it? Can you, or should you, be doing something about it? Is it within your control, or do you have to just deal with the consequences as well as you can?

- Think about your strengths, and any limitations and development needs. What has, and has not, worked for you previously?

- Where have you experienced real passion, commitment and a high level of achievement in a role? What can you learn from that experience? What roles did you really enjoy and why, or what parts of your current role do you really enjoy and do well?

- Where can your strengths, capabilities and attributes be deployed most appropriately? Are there areas that really matter? Which one or two areas, with a small investment, will make an exponential impact on your contribution, job satisfaction, or your options? What areas don't matter so much? Accept that these are not your strengths, nor are they likely to be, and so be it.

PART 2

LEAD OTHERS WITH RESOLVE

The second part of the book is about how we lead others through change, and draws more on the professional work we do. Leadership is a participatory sport and this means building the capabilities of others both individually and as a team. It means taking a fresh look at our biases, ensuring we create diverse teams and ways of thinking. Parts of this section draw on the approaches that my colleagues and I apply to help people to reflect on their careers, and to help organisations create and sustain great workplaces. We have developed the Arbiter Leadership Technologies consulting approaches and tools that are used by the NGS Global group in different parts of the world. We draw on, and acknowledge too, the great work of other thought leaders who have developed approaches and tools that we find particularly relevant.

16

TRANSFORMATIVE CHANGES NEED TRANSFORMATIVE LEADERS

Provide context and transparency through volatility and disruption

We used to talk about business as usual. Today, virtually every organisation we work with is going through significant change.

Commercial business models are greatly disrupted by those who have conceived and implemented new ways to solve problems or see services differently—just think of online and mobile financial services, parcel delivery, taxi services such as Uber and accommodation and booking services, whether aggregators or those made available through the sharing economy. In the public sector we, as citizens, are much less tolerant of overlapping services and slow response times. We want a one-stop shop and easy access online, just as we expect from other providers.

Today, providing context for others amidst volatility, dealing with ambiguity, and enabling digital transformation are key leadership capabilities. But sometimes too, we need to 'hasten slowly', know where we want to get to, and engage others in shaping that path and gaining success in a risk-managed way. As leaders, we need to provide context for those we lead, and accept that a significant part of our role is 'sense making' for others and that this is a learned skill.

Vice-Chancellor Jane Den Hollander received feedback from her team that the reason they liked working for her was that she 'simplified big problems into straightforward solutions'. She explains that her wiser, older self has come to understand that's what leaders do, 'They get involved in the intractable issues when their skills are needed.'

But it is not a gift, it is a learned skill. I would add that it improves with practice. We need to be sufficiently open and transparent, sharing what we know and being honest about what we don't. People appreciate honesty more than obfuscation and hiding the facts. The lack of openness about the situation of an organisation breeds distrust, suspicion and fuels rumour mills. As a friend once said to me about his workplace, 'Well if they don't tell us what is going on, we just have to make it up, and assume the worst'.

Some very effective executives we work with set up the expectation with their teams that there will be significant organisational changes at least every fifteen to eighteen months. This enables them to be responsive to the needs of their internal and external clients and to build a culture where change is not seen as a threat, but rather is the norm.

The Holling cycle provides a useful lens through which to view change

Sharing information as soon as it's available, and not sitting on bad news, has proved the most effective leadership technique for one of our clients.

In recent work with a client, we met with a mid-level executive we will call Sophie, as part of leadership capability and development. At one level there seemed to be nothing particularly remarkable or unusual about her approach to leading others. But, based on her responsibilities and work history, she had clearly been very effective in handling some very sensitive issues across several parts of her organisation and done this with a minimum of fuss.

We had good evidence of this from multiple inputs—her team, her peers and her manager. We found that what Sophie did differently from some of her peers was that she was totally honest with her team members, sharing information as soon as it was available for her to share. She did not sit on bad or negative news, but brought it out in the open. This built a great sense of trust in her team. They accepted that there were some things she could not share now, but would when she could, and they knew that she would do as she promised. Sophie learned too, to set the expectation that not too many organisations experienced very much of 'business as usual' these days.

The Holling Cycle or Adaptive Cycle (Holling, 2001), developed in the field of environmental economics and applied to organisations, is useful in providing context about how organisations change over time. This continuous cycle refers to four phases: conservation (business as usual, when things are balanced), release (where there is some form of crisis or disruption, a new threat or opportunity), renewal (the process of transforming to the new state) and then finally exploitation (where the organisations gains the benefits of transformation through deployment of new or refreshed resources, and growth).

In today's context, those business-as-usual periods tend to be shorter and shorter and the release cycle tends to happen more often. Transformation is required to move at a good pace, and the exploitation phase will also likely be shorter. To add to this, in most organisations, there will be multiple cycles happening concurrently across the organisation. This in turn increases the complexity we experience.

Thinking about these cycles provides a useful lens for understanding and explaining the sort of change situations we are currently experiencing.

Achieving digital transformation needs leadership transformation as a foundation

The quantum of change being driven by digital disruption demands a real and rapid evolution of leadership capabilities and behaviours, at all levels of our organisations.

Being able to move from being disrupted to using that disruption to improve experiences, communication, products and services requires some changes in how we lead.

It is useful to think of digital disruption—and the potentially beneficial outcome of digital transformation—as analogous to the large, external macroeconomic shifts and changes that are impacting economies. These cause disruption but, over time, enable growth and improvements in our standard of living, and in the health and education of populations.

On the micro side, these shifts have required changes in the importance of some leadership capabilities and behaviours to effect on the ground reform. These shifts are about how we lead ourselves and how we lead others.

So, what is different about the shifts we are currently experiencing—what is the impact of the quantum of the disruption?

The initial challenge is to appreciate that the quantum is very large, and that it has implications for every organisation.

In the words of John Chambers, CISCO Executive Chairman from 1995 to 2015, we are going through the 'biggest technology transition ever' (Chambers 2016). Rather sobering is his comment that we are only about one third through at this stage. One measure of the scale of change is that over the last twenty years, we have gone from about 1,000 Internet-connected devices, to over 500 billion. He declared that the technology component, whatever it is, is the 'easy part'.

The World Bank's 2016 *Digital Dividends Report* (World Bank 2016) makes a similar point—that gaining the benefits of digital developments requires 'analogue complements'. While the World Bank

Report was referring to broader economic policies and government action, our focus is more specifically on the analogue complements by way of the microeconomic reform of leaders and leadership.

Two areas stand out in relation to how leaders can be proactive towards digital disruption and hasten the path to transformation.

The first: emerging business and service models require greater agility, and that agility increases the importance of more networked and flexible people working together across and between businesses and organisations. Effective leaders focus on building these capabilities quickly.

The second: higher customer and citizen expectations have real implications for ongoing innovation. Fast-moving organisations understand and apply both diversity of thinking and practice, and truly agile methodologies, to how they evolve their services and products.

Agility requires networked and flexibility capabilities

As more traditional business and organisational models are increasingly disrupted through digital developments at a macro level, today's business and operating models are much more focused on working across organisations and across jurisdictions.

In the private sector, businesses that were once competitors now cooperate in agreed areas as advantages that mattered in previous times become commodities. Think of the back end of mortgage processing for example, or airline infrastructures and booking systems.

That ability to respond quickly, and in a more networked environment, requires agility, that is, the combination of speed and flexibility. Critical foundations for that agility are the capacity to trust and be trusted, and the ability to create effective teams.

Building trust is critical in leading others through volatile times.

As Stephen M.R. Covey so clearly articulates, trust is more than a social virtue (Covey 2008). Trust is an economic virtue too. Trust is about confidence, based on our belief in a person, or a team's, character and competence. The essence of character is our perspective on another's intent and integrity—for example, do they have good intent and do they do what they say they are going to do? The essence of competence is our perspective on another's capability and results—do they deliver the right things, and do this well?

Think about experiences of working with those you trust—things can happen more quickly. Recall your experiences working with those you don't trust. This tends to more painful, slower and not much fun.

Understanding and utilising the speed of trust enables people and organisations to exercise much greater agility in their actions. The same is true of effective teaming.

Building trust forms the basis of effective teams (Lencioni 2012). The starting point is people really getting to know each other as people, what motivates them and their strengths and vulnerabilities. It's about understanding and appreciating their intent, integrity, capabilities and the results they achieve—that is the 'trust thing' as described by Covey, mentioned above.

This provides the foundation then for overcoming the fear of conflict, the confidence to force clarity and closure, the ability to confront difficult issues and focus on collective outcomes.

Ongoing innovation increases the importance of our learning capabilities

Higher consumer and citizen expectations mean that leaders and organisations need to figure out how to be constantly innovating. Wilkinson refers to the evolution of generative leadership, where leaders see themselves as constant learners and innovators using ambiguity to find opportunities for new products and constructs (Wilkinson 2006).

As leaders we need to be able to co-design with others, inside and outside our organisations, to tackle issues with different perspectives. The diversity evident amongst the staff is critical here—diversity of thinking, backgrounds and experiences of cultures, genders, and life experiences. Like the speed of trust, diversity is more than social virtue. It fuels innovation. Lack of diversity constricts our thinking and our degrees of freedom to draw on different ways of viewing a challenge or issue.

Often our organisations have people who are real innovators, but they might be hidden in the organisational structure or bureaucracy. They might see things a bit differently, sometimes they are seen as 'problem employees', but if their capabilities are harnessed, and then appropriately protected, they can provide a rich vein of creativity.

Elisabet Wreme, now Chief Operations Officer with the Guild Group, worked in a number of organisations that had product development and innovation at their core, and then worked with a company that helped businesses commercialise technologies they developed. Some days it was mining technologies, sometimes information technologies and other days, medical developments. Her early learnings were that while every industry has its own peculiarities, there is much that is similar across industries and businesses.

The secret to her success was her curiosity, her ability to continue to ask questions while keeping in mind current and potential customer needs, and the financial and risk dynamics.

In the following sections I outline some significant changes that I have led or participated in. When I look back at the first example from the 1980s, there are many things I did not know or realise then, and a few I learned the hard way!

Initiating new developments requires engagement, commitment and pragmatism

Sometimes you need to prioritise pragmatism and forget your principles.

As a Senior Lecturer at RMIT in the mid-1980s, the then Departmental Head, Michael Ramsden, suggested I lead the preparation of a paper on the redevelopment of our initial professional programs and the development of new, potentially interdisciplinary, master's degree programs.

Michael was the sort of leader who gave his staff great encouragement and was not threatened by what might emerge from his younger colleagues.

We brought together a group of people from different departments and faculties and prepared the submission for a new Master of Business, which could have four or more specialist streams—Information Management, Business Systems/Information Technology, Computer Science and Engineering.

This required lots of documentation, and lots of stakeholder engagement, from each of the four faculties that were going to contribute to the new Master of Business—from up, down and across the university and from union representatives. That in itself was another great learning exercise.

We wanted the four faculties to put in a joint submission to the Academic Board, which would have been quite revolutionary at the time. But the university's processes only allowed for a single faculty to do this at any one time.

For a while I was stuck on the principle of the matter. Eventually the Vice-Chancellor took me aside and said, 'Just forget your principles and have your faculty propose it, making sure you have good support everywhere else'. That is what we did and it worked—it might have happened a bit sooner if I had been a bit more pragmatic earlier on.

When I became Head of Department, these changes led to the realisation that the future of our programs, and our department, would be best served by moving faculty.

We had worked closely with the Faculty of Business through the masters' developments and they seemed to have a greater understanding of our value, and the value of our graduates and programs, than our current faculty. But moving faculty was a much bigger decision than you might imagine, and turned out to be more controversial and demanding than I anticipated.

17

ACHIEVING CHANGE MEANS MANAGING RISKS

Leading change is often a double-edged sword, but worth the results

In the early stages of my career, I did not realise that what I found to be an entirely rational decision for a well-judged risk, others felt to be too big a step—emotionally and professionally.

Think of any business analogy you like—spinning off a business, selling your business to Private Equity or otherwise removing it from the ASX. Some saw it as a bit like telling your child to go live with another family.

In any such move, the risks and consequences need to be carefully gauged. As I have learned over the years, being comfortable with ambiguity is a key leadership capability.

One of the key risks at RMIT was our funding base. I needed to really understand the arcane, complex 'black box' of university funding: from Canberra, to the institution, to the faculties and then the department and its programs. This was one way to at least understand the level and nature of the risk and uncertainty we might be dealing with.

I became a bit of a headache for the university's Planning Officer. Nobody had asked these questions before, or, if they had, gave up more easily than I did. But I eventually got to understand the funding trail. It was like finding the end of the rainbow (without the pot of gold at the end). Each part of the funding chain had some form of formula. Some of our programs were classed as Applied Science, and some as Business, each had its own very different funding formula.

Business Faculty course funding was generally much lower than Applied Science, hence the biggest risk of moving faculty. So, moving meant understanding if our funding as a department came via the course (e.g. Master of Business) or the faculty in which we sat. It meant working with the Business Faculty to ensure that our funding base was not diminished over time (or at least not out of proportion to other diminishing funding).

In the end, the compromise struck was that for twelve months we would be part of both faculties and were expected to be at all the meetings of both. Think of it as somewhere between co-habitation and a trial marriage—with two partners concurrently. We were a department of less than twenty full-time academics so this was a big ask. But we did it, and then moved fully to the Business Faculty at the end of that year.

Lead change through gaining buy-in, taking risks, doing, learning and adapting

Managing change requires the occasional huge judgement call—anticipating what clients might be able to use effectively and providing services people did not know could help until they try them.

When I was invited to return to Gartner early in 2005 to be part of a major turnaround and lead new product development, none of us knew exactly what that meant. My first action was to start researching what was really meant by the term product development. I quickly realised I had been doing it for many years in different ways, I just didn't know that that was what it was called. We had input from market research, we had our own ideas and we led a lot of workshops internally teasing out the significant shifts that would make a quantum change to the business. We were developing role-based products and services—that is, shifting the company orientation from providing research that might be useful, to services targeted to what people actually do, every day.

As an aside, that comma before the 'every day' in the last sentence, took quite a while to evolve. Another of my learnings was working with serious marketing folks, and the importance of very succinct value proposition statements. We worked on that tagline—without the comma—for most of two days until we realised that the placement of the comma made all the difference.

Apologies if that seems trivial, but if you have been through this you will appreciate the sigh of relief, and joy even, when we figured it out.

Over time, we worked hard and well with our multiple constituencies—our executive colleagues, team members across the key groups of the Research, Consulting and Sales organisations, and of course our clients. We did the sort of research you would expect, but in the end there is always a big judgement call.

It's about anticipating what clients might be able to use effectively. We all know the example of market successes like Apple and Amazon where people were not necessarily clamouring for their products and services in advance. Rather, it is about creating a product or service that can shift how some basic things get done; it is about providing people with services they didn't know could help them, until they tried them.

Great leaders don't guard their pre-existing notions to the exclusion of new learnings

In the case of the Research organisation, we sought to change the nature of the work of hundreds of analysts—what they did and how they did it. This meant challenging more than six-hundred seriously smart people, who were mostly very experienced and used to doing what they did. But we needed to think of another way to provide what clients would want and thus turn the business around.

We started with one service line that had been controversial and not very successful to date, but we knew some of the key research analysts were quite passionate about these services. We got their buy-in to do things a bit differently, and then got the executive team across the line with the idea that it was really just a pilot—if it didn't work we could 'fail early' and rethink our approach. The leaders got it and, collectively, things started to shift gear.

There was one product line that we wanted to release but we lacked any real evidence of potential demand. This was in the area of Business Intelligence (and what is now more like Data Analytics). At the time there were few senior managers with that remit. One of our criteria for a new product was, in fact, to have a manager on the client's side allocated or dedicated to the product area. Without this, our Sales/Account teams would find it hard to locate the potential buyer for those services in an organisation. Today this area is related to that notion of 'Big Data' and 'Data Analytics' and how to get value from it, which is now top of many companies' concerns.

At the major client events, we invited clients to pre-book for some role-based workshops to help us clarify their issues across the eight role-focused services we were developing. Each of these so-called Business Intelligence Workshops were immediately the first to be booked out.

That judgement call turned out to very prescient, and a good lesson: sometimes the evidence isn't there, and you just have to be able to learn as you go along. Today we would call that being agile and adaptive, co-creating products and services with our clients.

Hastening slowly can help avoid being too far ahead

After a surprisingly sluggish pick up of new products by Gartner clients in Europe, we went on a 'listening' tour that uncovered a mesh of reasons behind this phenomenon.

Many Gartner products are not easy to sell because often they are intangible. Clients are not buying a new phone, or computer, a new staff member, or a new software product from which they can improve their profit. They are buying access to advice, participation in events or networking, and, ideally, gaining a level of assurance that when they need specific help it will be available by phone, video, via the web or in person.

That sort of scenario requires quite sophisticated Sales and Account professionals who are able to develop good relationships with senior clients. The business turnaround then meant a significant education and training program for our Sales teams. We had some big learnings here.

Our release schedule meant three new products each quarter (and we weren't the only part of Gartner now releasing new products).

We had faster take-up in North America compared to Europe, yet generally had more mature and senior Sales people across much of our European business. When we spent time with the European Sales team, they assured us that theirs was very much a relationship-based business. We would see the take-up, but not for a couple of months. They were right.

Some clients were a bit wary as we had launched products in the past that had then faded into the ether. These clients were going to 'wait and see', which was quite reasonable in the circumstances.

The final reason was particularly revealing. We were told that three products every quarter was a lot of products to learn about, and then introduce to clients. While they were delighted with the new products, we were, in fact, overwhelming the Sales teams. Even if they could get their heads around three different products, it was hard for them to introduce so many new things to multiple clients in the one quarter—and then there would be three more new products in the next quarter.

This was quite a wake-up call. We needed to both provide more support and also proceed more slowly. We coined the term 'hastening slowly' for what we needed to do over the next few months.

We stopped thinking about new things, slowed our release schedule, and put the time in to embedding those products we had released. We spent more time with Sales teams and went with them on more client calls. This worked and over the next six months the take-up passed our most optimistic projections.

Effective teamwork underpins turnarounds

Our goal in the first year was to halt the decline to a zero base. Instead we saw growth of three percent. By the end of year two we wanted ten percent growth and we were on track for eighteen percent.

It was the work of a lot of people—the executive team, sales leaders, our efforts in business and product development, marketing, and our research and consulting colleagues—focused on just a few things, relentlessly. None of us in the Business Development group were necessarily an expert in the areas for which we had taken accountability, but we did have some understanding of the culture of the company, client expectations for our services, and a willingness to try different things. We certainly made some mistakes, and we learned from those. Early on our timing was not quite right, and 'hastening slowly' made a big impact.

The nature of our team was critical. We were robust and opinionated individuals who built strong trust. We could have the difficult conversations and get over it. We rejected some of the 'facts' that didn't make sense to us and tried things out with our clients. We took them into our confidence about what we were trying to do and they worked with us. We made some judgement calls, learned from our mistakes, adapted and moved on.

We also celebrated our successes. We stopped to say 'Well done' or 'We did it' before taking breath and getting bogged down in the next thing. As a gross generalisation, that is one attribute that is more evident in US companies and something that is important to morale.

Today, as part of our interview processes with NGS, we often ask people about the best team they've been in (not led) as a team member. Most responses focus on a time-pressured situation where they worked on a turnaround, started a new program, or had to deliver a major new policy initiative.

It's when people have that shared vision, unity of purpose, and the ability to set aside their egos that they are the most focused and able to get things done.

Leading through disruption is the new normal

Leading organisations through disruption is difficult and leading them through digital disruption to digital transformation is not for the faint-hearted, but it is the new normal. Businesses, government agencies, educational institutions and just about all organisations experience disruption from technology developments, such as the impact of mobile communications, social media, new forms of payments and different consumer or citizen expectations. But then the challenge is to use this disruption, and use the technologies that make sense to deliver better services or products. That is how disruptions that we might not have much control over can be harnessed to transform, uplift or just improve what our organisations do and how they do it.

The foundations of leadership remain critical—curiosity and understanding of the environment, the ability to shape a vision based on multiple variables, competence in financial dynamics, the confidence and authenticity to inspire and lead others, and good self-knowledge.

Leading others today and tomorrow also places much greater emphasis on the need for adaptability, providing context for others, being able to implement agility with trust and effective teaming, and creating a culture of, and expectation for, change and innovation.

18

BUILDING TRUST DELIVERS
GREAT WORKPLACES

Trust changes everything

Trust has always been fundamental to our personal and professional relationships but the ability to develop and sustain trust amongst teams and in organisations is now widely recognised.

The ability to trust, and be trusted, enables us to work more quickly and with a greater sense of accomplishment. That is quite a claim, but underpinning this is Stephen M.R. Covey's articulation of the notion that, 'Trust is more than a Social Virtue'.

Before starting to work more closely in the leadership capability and executive search area, trust was always important to me—building it, its presence and absence. However, I would have struggled to really grasp how to describe it, its different components, and the levers that can improve—or undermine—it.

Trust might have had something of a jelly-like quality—hard to really grasp, to define, and to understand its many dimensions. You know when you experience it, and you know when it is not there. A year or so ago, I had the opportunity to re-acquaint myself with Stephen M. R. Covey, and his work *The Speed of Trust* (2008) as facilitator for his major Australian business commitments. Stephen Jr. is the son of Stephen R. Covey, author of the ubiquitous *7 Habits of Highly Effective People* (1989). Stephen Covey Jnr ended up leading his father's business and then the merged entity FranklinCovey, as CEO.

Covey makes a strong case that the ability to trust—and be trusted—changes everything. Where we trust another person, or members of our team, or our boss, or those from another organisation, we can get on with things much more quickly. The speed of trust enables us to speed up our interactions and the nature and quality of our links with others.

If we have a trusting relationship with another person, we have confidence in dealing with them, that they will do what they say they are going to do, and that they have the willingness and capacity to do the right thing.

Trust has economic value and reduces the cost of interactions

Trust is much more than a social virtue. Trust has economic value in that it is an asset that reduces your interaction time and your transaction costs.

When trust goes up, speed goes up and costs go down. It is a critical factor in the development and success of effective leaders and smart organisations.

Lack of trust fosters a climate of suspicion and saps your energy as you start double-guessing situations and often doing 'workarounds'. As Covey puts it, 'Mistrust doubles the cost of doing business'.

In our work we often ask candidates or executive participants in leadership advisory work— 'Who's the best boss you have ever had?' or 'What's the best peer team you have ever been part of?'

We are seeking to understand the sort of work environment where they really thrive, but the reasons behind their answer tend to be consistent. We get responses such as 'We trusted each other to get things done', 'We trusted each other to do the right things' or 'I felt really trusted by others, and I really enjoyed that and gave it everything'.

But what is this thing called trust? We might instinctively know that it is a good thing, but Covey's real contribution is to elucidate what trust is, its key components, why they matter, and what you can do about it.

Character and competence *together* enable us to trust and be trusted

We trust another person when we have confidence in them. That trust, says Covey, is based on another's perception of your character and your competence. Both are required for us to really trust others.

About character: intent plus integrity

Covey provides a neat analogy of a large tree. It has deep roots, powerful branches and continues to grow. The roots and trunk are about the character of the tree—demonstrating integrity and intent.

We have all come across people who are technically competent, and whose expertise was much valued by their organisation, but they were not trusted. They might be smart and know a lot about the business, or the program or products, but their behaviour was not consistent with what was required. Perhaps they did not collaborate well, or share information with others, or were not respectful of the work of others. They were competent, but lacked good intent, and thus lacked integrity. We did not trust them because of their character.

Integrity is simply defined as the congruence between your intent and the behaviour you exhibit. A person of high integrity is someone who does what they say they are going to do—their intent is actioned in their behaviour.

About competence: capabilities plus results

The upper part of the tree, the branches that produce the fruits or flowers, represent our competence. Competence is about your capabilities and your results. Your talents, skills, knowledge, capacities and abilities go together to make up your capabilities. These are your foundation. Results are about your track record or what you have actually achieved, and results matter to your credibility.

We can all recall colleagues who have demonstrated good character as evidenced in their integrity and good intent. But those two elements are not enough for us to fully trust them if they can't get the job done because they don't have the capabilities to get the job done, or don't apply these well to deliver the necessary results.

If we think our colleagues are not competent, then we are not likely to really trust them to see through the completion of a difficult job. We know that it would put ourselves or others at risk.

As an aside, it is always a powerful and positive sign when those with good expertise, but bad behaviours—and who have been warned and failed to reform—are exited from an organisation. It can be a turning point reinforcing the expectations and behaviours that will, and will not, be rewarded.

To sum up: trust is about character (intent plus integrity) and competence (capabilities plus results).

Practice the reciprocity of trust

While trust can be described as a tangible attribute and asset, gaining and giving trust can remain a challenge. Trust is a reciprocal virtue— that is, we need to trust others to get trust in return.

We all know people who are gullible and have trusted too many people, and we know those who are overly suspicious and who trust no-one. Being overly trusting is probably better than being overly suspicious. The positivity created by trusting others is a powerful leadership tool.

Most people come to work to do a good job. They want to do the right thing. But we each have our own personal and particular ways of processing how others have acted, or how we perceive they have acted. Our own experiences and the lens through which we view the world can get in the way sometimes.

Assume good intent on the part of others, don't sweat the small stuff

A key learning for me over the years has been to always assume goodwill and good intent on the part of others.

If there is a choice between conspiracy and stuff-up, I assume stuff-up every time, and ninety-five percent of the time that is the reality. This translates to how you think about those who have said or done something that is potentially hurtful or harmful. It is best to assume good intent and then probe, with them, where the misunderstanding came in.

Recently, in working with an executive team, we spent some time on understanding the real and practical dimension of trust. This was after some work on them truly getting to know each other—as that is essential for trust.

Members of the team were asked to share their tendencies in relation to a range of areas of trusting behaviours—their key strength and an area they really needed to work at.

Because of the nature of this group, we were encouraging people to assume good intent in others as a starting point. It was quite transformative of relationships amongst the group, whose roles were quite interdependent.

We had great feedback from the team, including some months later as this way of illuminating trust had been helpful. The team had a shared understanding and shared language to discuss some difficult behavioural issues, and trust was now something about which they could talk openly.

A couple of months after a workshop one of the group members spoke about how this impacted his professional and personal relationships. He was the legal counsel and explained that he had been raised and educated to be suspicious. When he started ascribing good intent as the starting point for any discussion or negotiation, he found it changed the whole dynamic and good things happened more quickly. He also explained that he was now applying this at home too and it had made quite a difference in his family relationships.

In my own case, my brain is wired for rational and logical thinking and, over time, it has had to contend with a lot of inputs that are neither. Years ago, if someone did something that seemed not so logical, I might have thought there was an underlying reason for that—perhaps something quite negative. Now I will (mostly) assume some form of misunderstanding, crossed wires, or a time zone or sleep deprivation matter. This combination of directness and assuming good intent saves a lot of heartburn and angst.

Of course, we each need to have a level of cultural sensitivity here. I have spent a lot of time in different countries, including those in parts of Asia where, at first encounter, people's views might seem more opaque. You have to take your cues from others, but there are ways to be polite and direct at the same time, and I have found it is usually appreciated.

In working so much in the US I learned too about speaking in euphemisms. Most Americans are unfailingly polite—to a fault. My careful bluntness had to be tempered early on, but I believe many colleagues found it more satisfying and productive to be direct and sort out any misunderstandings quickly, rather than letting them linger or fester. Sometimes we just have to let a few things go and not sweat the small stuff. There are so many bigger things for us to be concerned about. If something is not really material, then just let it go. It is about choosing which battles to fight and realising there is only so much airtime available. We each need to use it well and on things that really matter.

It is worth keeping in mind when you reflect on your own approach to trusting others. Our ability to trust, and be trusted by, others is part of the fabric of organisational cultures—the way we do things around here.

19

BEHAVIOURS REFLECT REAL VALUES

Executive behaviours reveal the real values of an organisation

How often have you been in a boardroom and seen a statement of 'Our Values' on the wall? How often have you wondered… who cares?

If you are like me, you wonder what weight is really put on these. How did they come about? Were they generated by some consultants, or do they really represent what this organisation is really striving for?

Some years ago, a colleague and I walked into a boardroom to start work with a CEO and an executive team. We noticed their values exhibited on a poster on the wall, but it seemed to us that their behaviour did not reflect these. When we indicated this, in reasonably diplomatic language, we were informed that that was just something that the marketing and human resources folks had developed a while ago.

We suggested they take it down and work on something that really engaged staff—our experience is that more than ninety percent of people have good insights into what is, and is not, working.

Values created by someone else can be a more negative than positive activity—especially if they do not reflect the reality of people's experiences. And it is worse if the CEO and members of the executive team do not exhibit those values.

An organisation's cultural values seriously shape how it performs and how difficult it is, or is not, to shift and change or evolve to face new and different situations. There is a greater sense of reality that values do matter. Just think about the recent history of Google or Facebook, or recent developments and reporting about our larger financial institutions.

Values underpin 'how work gets done around here' and how people behave and are treated at work. It's important for your individual health and well-being to be part of an organisation where there is some congruence in your personal values and your organisation's values.

The Barrett Cultural Values Audit helps uncover organisation values

In the work we do with executives and teams, we often seek to understand an organisation's values—both the reality of what exists today and what people would like them to be.

Think of this as three different perspectives on values: those of the individual staff members, the current values exhibited in the organisation, and the values that are important for the future.

One approach we use is the Cultural Values Audit approach (Barrett 2017 and Barret Values Centre on the Reference list), and some of the tools that go with this, to help us work with teams to clarify current values and then have executive teams, or perhaps the whole organisation, focus on the most critical values that really matter to their future organisation.

This process is engaging, and the outcome helps identify the gap between current values and those that you really want to see exhibited in the future. It enables organisations to really focus on no more than two or three values that most people in the team or organisation really want to see embedded in how they work.

Through some simple but well-developed online tools, organisations of anywhere between about 10 and 50,000 people can engage in this process, and the approach has even been applied through sampling techniques to many nations. But let's get back to organisations.

We have been using this CVA approach with commercial, public sector, not-for-profit and educationally focused organisations over many years.

Revealing the gap between current and desired values enables a clear focus

While working recently with a team in the not-for-profit sector, we found the leadership group clearly lacked cohesiveness. One executive expressed this, 'I am not sure we have the same shared values, goals and expectations of each other. If unresolved there is a risk that the team will become more dysfunctional'.

This executive team had real issues in differences of opinions in some major decisions they had to make. In the end the CEO did what we have now come to know as a 'Captain's call'. However, that left residual damage amongst a group of people who were committed to their organisation and its constituency.

The organisation was not 'broken' and was performing well in its market, but the executive team needed to be able to deal with difficult issues and manage conflicts more productively. They did not want the cracks that they had recently experienced to widen, but they knew that they were not strong, as a team, in putting the difficult issues on the table. Our job was to help them understand why, and to enable them to work through those issues in a robust and constructive way.

One of the approaches we used in working with them was a Values Audit. We worked with them to identify their own personal values, those they saw currently in the organisation and those they really wanted to see.

The results, and resulting discussions, proved pivotal in

understanding why they were having some issues and what they needed to do about that. Through the Values Audit, the group identified many positive values in their current environment, including teamwork, a results orientation, quality and integrity. Amongst the more negative values they identified were too much bureaucracy, a silo mentality, internal competition, and a confused future focus.

The top four desired values were trust, respect, commitment and accountability. Commitment was the only one of these four in the current top 10 exhibited values and it was number eight.

The next step was to clarify what people really meant by those words—trust, respect, commitment, and accountability—and we did this through a carefully facilitated workshop.

This was a way of elucidating current behaviour that people considered to be less than appropriate, and the sort of behaviour they really wanted to see in each other. It also served as a first step in walking through how to have those difficult conversations and deal constructively with the sub-terrain conflicts that were being avoided.

Robust conversations are important in organisations, but the prerequisite for their success is an environment of mutual trust. We did this in two tranches.

1. Clarifying the meaning of the values of trust and respect

The group worked through what trust meant to them and agreed on the following meaning:

> When there is a high level of trust, we have the confidence that each of us has the intent, capability and integrity to do the right thing by each other and the organisation, and that we are open with each other.

While the meaning of respect had something of a biblical tone to it, the group agreed that the words below reflected their agreed collective views:

> When there is a high level of respect we treat others as we would wish to be treated—as valued professionals who might have different perspectives and opinions—and always assume goodwill and positive intent.

My experience is that the notion of assuming goodwill and positive intent is a hurdle that, once overcome, enables different types of interactions.

2. Clarifying the meaning of the values of commitment and accountability

Sometimes people express dissatisfaction with the level of commitment of their peers or team members and want to see that really strengthened.

When that is the case, it can be because expectations have not been clarified or shared. That was the situation in the NFP organisation. Their perspective on commitment then was that:

> When there is a high level of commitment, we meet agreed expectations for our role and the organisation in terms of effort, priorities, time, energy and positive impact, and we also acknowledge and accept the need to balance personal and professional commitments.

Accepting and implementing accountability is a major issue in most sectors. This is about holding yourself, your peers and your team members accountable for whatever it is they have agreed to do or should be doing. The explanation of accountability was that:

> When there is a high level of accountability, we agree on what we are each going to do, we do it, and others can and will hold us accountable for that.

About the hardest thing to do sometimes is to hold your peers accountable, to be able to have a frank conversation about where, in your view, they have disappointed you by failing to deliver to clients or each other.

It is hard to do that in a constructive and straightforward way if there is not a good level of trust and respect amongst a peer team.

We get back to the point here that building trust, as mentioned earlier, is the most critical aspect of creating great teams, and it requires deliberate work to get there.

It is worth pondering—what do you think is the gap between the values your organisation espouses, and the ones that you experience? What do your peers and team members think? What can you do about that?

20

SUCCEED WITH GREAT TALENT AND TEAMS

Grow your talent from within to keep the right people

The last time your organisation had a vacancy in the C-suite, how was the quality of candidates. Did the internal and external talent compare?

Quite often we hear that there is no one inside the organisation who could do the job and that is sometimes true. But it is worth asking—why is that the case? Sometimes organisations are small, with unique characteristics and it would be hard for an executive team member to take on that role without putting the organisation at risk.

In larger organisations though, this should not be the case. There are plenty of opportunities for good mobility. Providing up-and-coming talent with diverse experiences and work on good stretch projects should be just part of their development.

The key is to make the most of the talent you have. This might sound strange coming from someone who helps organisations to source external executive talent. However, our focus is very much making leadership teams the best they can be, and that means each of us getting the most value from the staff we already have.

For many organisations there is no magical access to a large external talent pool. Every external appointment brings with it some risk. Research clearly indicates this is a bigger risk than internal candidates, or at least those who might have worked for your organisation previously. Moreover, constantly bringing in new external people can have a very demoralising effect on those who thought that there could be a good career path in the organisation.

If leaders and managers are doing their jobs well the talent should be there and it should be nicely evolving at each level. Building the capability of your people, giving them some good stretch goals while at the same time being sufficiently supportive, is what good leaders do.

This should be the case in every type of organisation whether it is a small or large business, a local, state or federal government agency or department, or an educational institution.

Let's say Sandra and Sam are direct reports to a senior executive. Each is keen to gain experience in another area of your department or business, or wants an industry secondment, or even an opportunity for further study. They have come to you as their executive manager to discuss their options. You can only afford to have one out at the time. It's quite likely that you will choose the one that presents the least risk—most often, where there is another team member who can step into their place, whom they have been developing for just such an eventuality.

Talent management is not an optional extra for leaders

While you need some injection of external talent from time to time, it is critical to develop and nurture the talent you have. In some developmental work we did in one organisation, we recommended that one of the senior managers (who we will call Trang) be offered a secondment to another line of business to develop her P/L. Trang worked in finance but really needed some line-management experience.

Her manager's first questions to Trang were along these lines: 'If you take a secondment elsewhere for say, twelve to eighteen months, who is ready to do your job? Who is it, on your team, who is on track for a more senior role, and we can support during that period? How many internal candidates will there be if we take expressions of interest, and what will be the risk or trade-off with each person?' Do you know the answer to those questions yourself if you were in that situation?

In advising executives and managers we have asked these questions many times. Too often people blanch and mutter something about the fact that putting a serious focus on succession planning was something they were going to do, but there were always more urgent priorities.

In advising an executive manager on his career he noted that he wanted to move interstate and broaden his role in the organisation. We asked him about his team and he assured us they were great as he had hired most of them himself over the past two years. Then we asked him some further questions, 'what is your succession plan?' and 'who can step into the role you are currently doing?'

He quickly responded that, well, no one could do that. He acknowledged that there was a big gap between himself and his direct reports, and that he had not thought about potential succession in his recruitment process.

Effective succession planning means managing, nurturing, pushing and prodding your talent, that is, those who report to you, your broader team, and in many cases your peers. It's about tracking their progress and development and knowing when they are really ready for the next big project, or even the next challenge, that will demonstrate to them, and to you, how they are progressing.

There is plenty of recent and credible research on the impact of consistent, thoughtful and rigorous talent management on both organisational performance and retention of those the organisation is most keen to keep.

Great talent will go to where it is valued and can thrive

Talent management is now an everyday must do. Smart organisations realise this and act on it.

They know that often their employees have higher and more demanding expectations for personal growth and opportunities than they had, say, ten years ago. They know how critical it is to demonstrate that there is a real future for staff here. They take their obligations for development seriously, and it is noticed throughout the organisation.

If staff see that the vacant roles always go to external talent, it can be demoralising. What is the point of working hard here if there is no career path? That career path involves at least a great focus on ongoing development—and rewarding those who undertake relevant self-initiated and, in some cases, self-funded development.

While it is one of those findings that seems incongruous, where employees believe they are being developed, and are marketable, they are more likely to remain with an organisation. They don't have to leave to gain development or maintain their professional currency elsewhere.

Government and not-for-profit organisations are usually less likely to be able to offer higher-level competitive financial rewards, but they are able to offer great development opportunities through a serious and considered approach to how they manage talent.

If you want that talent to be part of your team—and remain part of your team for at least a reasonable time—it requires a serious and genuine focus on knowing and growing the capabilities of the individuals and the team that you have.

Creating great teams is hard but rewarding work

The level of teamwork in the office is one of the key factors in staff either wanting to stay, or being interested when other opoortunities arise elsewhere. How would you describe the attributes of the team of which you are a member (not the team you lead)? Would you use words like 'effective, cohesive, supportive and committed'? Or would descriptions like 'lacking in trust', 'not really a team or truly collaborative' and 'engaging in conflict avoidance' be more appropriate? If we asked the same question of the team you lead, how would your team members describe their experiences as a member of your team?

Great teams don't just happen. They are the result of a lot of effort from the team leader and each team member. They are usually the outcome of a conscious and deliberate effort to understand what makes teams work well, and learn what matters to the individual members (and acknowledge this in tangible ways). This is complemented by good linkage between individual aspirations and roles to the remit of the organisation.

The path to achieving truly effective teams is not rocket science and it is well documented. So why do so many of us have experiences of mediocre, frustrating, or just plain bad teamwork?

The answer lies in the simple failure to build genuine trust amongst team members, to build the trust that individuals need to really get to know one another as people. They need to know what matters to each other, to deal with conflict constructively, agree on commitments and then hold each other accountable for delivering agreed results.

This sounds simple, and at one level it is. But first, each of us needs to be willing to come to terms with two things: the first is to understand ourselves, and the second is to really get to know, and understand, our colleagues as people—rather than as just another officer, peer, executive, manager or service provider.

About six months ago we were in conversation with a newly appointed executive responsible for a large team of smart people providing services to many significant commercial executives, government departments and agencies.

The executive, we will call Ben, was thrilled with his appointment, but aware that he had inherited a competitive and challenging group of smart individuals, focused on achieving their individual goals. Ben had heard comments that it takes at least eighteen months to build a really great team and wanted to know if this was true. We explained that that is about the usual time period, but you can certainly accelerate this process with a sound grasp of the importance of building trust, modelling trusting behaviour, personal focus, real consistency and commitment.

That consistency and commitment starts with the leader of the team, and their ability to share their strengths, weaknesses, development needs and experiences with the team they lead. There are risks here, but without some informed risk-taking the rewards don't come.

Sharing vulnerabilities builds trust

When we take on our early executive or management roles, we often want to show ourselves to be strong, truly capable, and lacking in vulnerabilities. But some of the most powerful and effective leaders adopt a different stance: they share what matters to them as an individual, not just as an executive. They know their strengths and where they need help and they are not afraid to share that with their team members. They are also willing to share their failures, what they learned from them, and areas that they continue to work on.

Their real strength is their ability to build trust by trusting their team members with information about their own vulnerabilities. They are modelling the behaviour that they want their team members to demonstrate.

This is not necessarily easy and can be misunderstood. Our perceptions of gender differences and different cultural expectations complicate this situation. But the ability to model real trust and, through that, have other team members trust each other, is the foundation of great teamwork.

We have worked with, and observed, a significant number of executive leaders and their teams who have taken that journey in different ways.

Some years ago, I was part of a global team where we managed to get together face-to-face about every three months (remembering too, that this was years before Skype, Halo or Telepresence). My younger boss, Robin, mentioned in earlier chapters, had a keen focus on us getting to know more about each other. We got to understand each other's backgrounds, where and how we grew up, our outside interests and commitments, and our personal values and drivers.

At the time I felt this was quite enjoyable but perhaps a bit diverting as it took time from the real business of our meetings. However, I came to appreciate how quickly we were getting to know and appreciate each other, be comfortable with how we each got things done, and our different personalities and quirks (of which there were quite a few). That understanding of each other, our strengths and vulnerabilities, was critical during some quite tough times, as well as the speed with which we had to lead and deliver change.

The experience of that team remains with me today as we were able to then more readily deal with conflicts, have very direct discussions, agree on commitments and expect that these would be delivered as agreed with each of us doing our parts. We held each other accountable for what we had agreed to do.

Again, it is worth reflecting, how would your team members describe their experiences as a member of your team? Do you know? Have you asked them?

21

LEADERSHIP IS A PARTICIPATORY SPORT

Focus early on team member capability and development

Self-knowledge is critical to effective leadership and is a key ingredient in great teams. Really knowing who you are, being comfortable with that and being willing to share your vulnerability is the first step in building trust with others.

It's hard to develop an individual's capabilities if you don't understand where they are right now. This is even more critical when you have come in as a new executive or manager, or the organisation has a new remit.

We find that people who have not been such good performers under one manager might greatly improve with a different type of leadership. In that situation, it is important to get to the essence of an individual's drivers, their track record and their potential.

If the organisation is involved in some kind of reorganisation, the people currently in place might not be well matched to those new roles, but they could be with some capabilities development. This can be tough but we find most individuals are very much aware of how they are tracking, and whether or not they will survive and thrive in the new environment.

Where the change doesn't work, a well-positioned and well implemented individual capability and development needs assessment—conducted with their input and with care and respect—usually helps people move on with dignity and greater knowledge of the roles where they will do well (and, usually, be happier).

We often assume we know a lot about the individuals on our team and that they know a lot about each other. Our experience is that spending time early on to really understand the capabilities, motivations, experience and development needs of team members is a worthwhile investment.

The sponsoring executive or team leader of course also participates fully and has the opportunity to grow through the process of a better shared understanding about the dynamics of the team.

Know what you're great at, then ensure the rest is good enough

It is about knowing what you are great at, and then ensuring you are good enough in other areas that matter. A key part of this process is being transparent and open, with no 'black box' or 'gotcha' components. It is about really getting to know yourself, your strengths and areas for improvement that matter (acknowledging that some areas just don't matter so much, depending on the role).

Getting to know the capabilities and development needs of individual team members is best explained by way of an example: A client we will call Ellen, was appointed as the new service delivery manager in an established agency. She needed a quick understanding of her team and approached us about this. We gave her feedback on the organisational and structural changes she was intending to make.

When she settled on the first phase of new organisational arrangements and revised positions, we worked with her broader team in several workshops to develop position descriptions and an organisation-specific, then role-specific, set of Capability Frameworks.

A Capability Framework is much more than a wish list of generic leadership attributes. It specifies in concrete terms the technical/professional, management and leadership requirements for a role.

The biggest gap we find is usually in the specification of the capabilities: for example, the experience, track record and transferable attitudes and behaviours that a particular role requires.

Roles that might look similar often are not. They might have different types of governance, stakeholders, customer-facing demands, union engagement, communication or political dimensions. Different levels of ambiguity, regulatory frameworks and the ability to escalate (or not) are also often important.

In the case of Ellen's group, each member of the team, and then many of their direct reports, was included in a process to understand their track record and potential, particularly in light of the new structure, focus and positions. They then each received considered feedback, and an actionable individual Development Plan.

Adults talking with adults: a critical component of development

A key part of the processes we lead is a face-to-face conversational interview that draws heavily on the attributes required for a particular role. We refer to this as 'adults talking with adults'.

At a certain level, people need the opportunity to share their experiences and expertise in a well conducted 'guided' conversation, using good behavioural interviewing techniques. Although not a replacement, the use of psychometrics, such as emotional intelligence assessments, can be useful to support that process.

In the case of Sophia's team, of the seven roles that became the new roles reporting to the CEO, four were immediately appointed from the previous leadership team. Three were the subject of an external search resulting in two new executives joining the team and one was filled by a promotion from the next level down.

This represented a good mix of internal and external talent, where the internal talent had really demonstrated, during this and other processes, that they were ready to co-lead in a different way. Each member of the broader team, these executives and their direct reports, had a clear notion of their strengths and development needs or where they needed to improve to be good enough. And they had a pathway to get there if they were willing and able to invest the time and energy.

Working outside your comfort zone can be important for development

A frequent recommendation when we work on development plans for individuals is that the individual needs to broaden his or her experience.

For example, in a commercial context, we often see the need for both emerging and established leaders to take on roles outside their comfort zone. This is particularly important where you have people who have been mostly in corporate roles, such as human resources, finance, information technology, legal or compliance, rather than, say, a line of business with full P/L accountability.

In a public sector context, we have regularly recommended that those with strong policy backgrounds take on an operational role for eighteen to twenty-four months. It doesn't mean they will become the world's best operational leaders, but it does mean they will develop a much stronger understanding of the implications of policy and what it actually takes to execute what looks like a rational policy position.

As leadership advisors we are often asked if we coach individuals who need some assistance in a particular area. Our usual response is to indicate that we will certainly work with an individual to help them gain greater self-knowledge, understand their capabilities, strengths and areas for development, and work with them on an actionable and pragmatic individual development plan. This brings about considerable professional and personal development in the participant.

Develop and apply well-targeted and pragmatic capability frameworks

Many leading commercial and public sector organisations are rethinking how they assess capabilities for future executives and managers in an environment of shifting needs, considerable ambiguity and volatility.

The specific needs in particular roles might go in a quite different direction due to factors such as market pressures, technology shifts changing the nature of a business, a change of government policy, or maybe the scope of the role being too big in the first place. Some of us, me included, have had the opportunity of being appointed to roles that did not exist before. This is usually a great opportunity, if you are the type of person who is good at figuring out what really needs to be done, and then convincing your boss and your peers, and perhaps your clients also, that this is what you should do.

Quite a few of the Executive Search roles we've worked on are new or completely reshaped roles. Think of the number of times you have come across newish roles like Chief Customer Experience Officer, Transformation Lead, Employee Experience Executive, Chief Digital Officer and Data Analytics Executive.

When working with groups on Executive and Team Development, the focus is on what the organisation really needs from its leaders in the future. Part of the challenge then is working out what real capabilities are needed to successfully fulfil specific executive and management roles.

This can often cause considerable debate—and it is meant to do so. It surfaces 'what really matters around here' now, and in the future, in an open and transparent way, so that the group itself recommends, and thus owns, those capabilities.

What capabilities do corporate executives require?

We separate capabilities into three big buckets. They include: professional, managerial and leadership.

Professional: learning orientation and career relevance

Professional capabilities focus on learning orientation and career relevance. Where is evidence of your learning progression and your career track record? It is about what you have achieved to date, and your process of continued learning and application of that learning. This will include your level of functional capability, and your broader knowledge and understanding of the organisation and role.

Once you have about fifteen years in the workforce, the key guide to what you can achieve is likely to be found in what you have done to date. A multiplier, though, will be your level of curiosity and the extent to which you are a continuous learner.

Managerial: strategic acuity and execution excellence

Managerial capability is about strategic acuity and execution excellence. It is about how you think about problems, their context and time horizon, the ability to see implications, plus how you get things done. It is about how you make decisions and deliver value to your organisation or clients. How you deal with ambiguity and uncertainty, and with complex problems. What is the evidence for your political 'nous' and your ability to prioritise—to do the right things at the right time?

Organisations are often looking for people who are agile in their thinking—who can unlearn what they know and then relearn different ways of getting things done.

Recently the term VUCA has been coined to describe the situation faced by many organisations—volatility, uncertainty, complexity and ambiguity.

Increasingly a key capability is to understand context, or as one organisation called it—organisational and situational awareness. This was about how individuals were able to shape and frame recommendations and decisions based on a firm understanding of the organisation's shift in focus, its new remit, and the broader political environment.

A few years ago, in working with a large commercial organisation, the participants added 'global business perspective' to their capabilities as all executives and managers have to be totally attuned to international commercial realities.

Leadership: character and resolve

Leadership capabilities include your character and resolve—how you lead yourself, and your ability to lead others. This is really the key to your potential as an executive leader.

Consider the following: In leading others, where have you been able to build and develop effective teams, implement accountability, and be persuasive and influential? To what extent do you operate in an open and transparent manner? Where have you received a real knockback, a disappointment or perhaps failed to deliver to your own expectations? How did you deal with this? What have you learned from working with difficult stakeholders?

What capabilities do public sector executives require?

We have worked with the Australian Department of Prime Minister and Cabinet and the Public Service Commission on Secretary succession planning.

One of our first tasks was to develop a capability framework specifically for Departmental Secretaries (the CEOs of major government agencies). We sought input from the key stakeholders, including past Secretaries and senior bureaucrats to complete this.

Attributes identified as critical for senior public sector executives included good initial qualifications and a record of personal learning and development. Next was track record, or what they had delivered that was difficult to do and that required strong and effective stakeholder engagement, and who would attest to that. Who could they name as referees, and to what extent did their peers hold these referees in high regard? Personal qualities included presence, which incorporated areas such as confidence and assertiveness, integrity and energy.

The ability to lead by managing relationships and collegiality was important. As was being comfortable with ambiguity and complexity, while also being flexible and agile. Demonstrating good judgement was a must. Finally, there was the ability to provide policy advice and service delivery, and to prioritise and be accountable.

Of course, it is hard—if not impossible—to find all these qualities at a very high level in one individual.

That's why, when faced with say twelve to fifteen capabilities, we work with executive or management teams to have the team select the top three. This in itself is a great exercise.

Our experience is that most groups will agree on one, and after that there is a broader spread. We then focus on facilitating a robust discussion about 'what really does matter around here' in relation to future executive needs.

As another client of ours commented, if he got nothing more out of the process of executive and team capability work than a much greater understanding of each member of his team, then it was very worthwhile. At the end, his team walked away with better knowledge of each other, and also themselves.

Build teams with shared values but complementary capabilities

We are currently helping a number of long-term clients to build teams that have the right mix of experience, capabilities and attributes.

For this we need to consider diverse backgrounds, experiences and where they are on the spectrum of embracing change, noting that each team needs a good mix of change catalyst or originators— those who are good pragmatists seeking to clarify the purpose and expected outcomes of change, and those who have propensity to originate change.

It is worth asking the question—in your organisation, what level of agreement and shared understanding is there about the key capabilities executives and managers need for your future organisation's success?

This reinforces the importance of really knowing your peers, your team members and then working at building deep teaming capabilities. It means sharing your vulnerabilities too.

22

RETHINK OUR LENSES.
TAKE A FRESH LOOK AT BIAS

Gender stereotyping starts very early on

In many areas, as boys and girls grow up, we continue to treat them quite differently, to set different expectations and to use different language in our interactions.

My personal experience with the birth and early development of our fourth child brought this home to me in a big way. Robert and I have three sons and a daughter, Katie, who was the last-born. We had always wanted to have four children—we both come from large families and four seemed like something of a compromise. We were not 'going for the girl' in that fourth pregnancy and, in fact, I was expecting to have four boys, and that would have been fine.

So when Katie was revealed as a girl, that was actually a bit of a surprise to me. But what came as much more of a surprise was the entirely different reaction I experienced from hospital staff and (some) friends and (some) relatives. It was the interaction of people with a baby girl that stunned me, and this continued as she grew. My observation would be that every day, there were little things, different ways of interacting, that I had just not seen with young boys. It included different ways of speaking, people adjusting their voices, and assuming that more inanimate or passive toys were appropriate, rather than action or interactive toys. This would later include assumptions about behaviours, more limited sporting options, different approaches to musical interests or entertainment, or just lower expectations for achievements, for speaking up, and contributing to conversations.

In the working environment, multiple factors influence the disparity between the prevalence of women and men in management and executive roles. There are three that I come across regularly, in both executive search and working with organisations on leadership capability and talent management.

The first relates to how women often approach opportunities, the second is the different perceptions of similar behaviour between women and men, and the third is how women and men tend to articulate and 'own' their achievements.

Women need to assume they can do it

Often men will assume they meet the criteria for a new role and should apply. Yet most women tend to be far more circumspect and are less likely to apply (as I was myself, as mentioned in an earlier chapter). I use the term 'most' here judiciously, as my experience is that this is the case with at least eighty percent of women, and much lower percentage of men, perhaps about fifteen to twenty-five percent.

While this situation is changing, we see it regularly when proactively contacting women we believe should or could be a candidate for a particular role. The response often is: 'But I don't understand. What makes you think I could do that?', something that we hear much less often from men at the same stage in their career.

It's time to remove the different filters we put on women and men's behaviours

The second challenge is about the different perceptions of similar behaviour between men and women. We see this most overtly in the political sphere, where women's behaviour is seen through a very different lens from men's behaviour. It's time to refresh our gender lenses.

The most succinct commentary I have seen on this situation comes from Barbra Streisand who, as well as being a wonderfully talented performer, is also an astute businessperson.

In October 2012, *Harvard Business Review* published an interview with Barbra as a high-performing business leader. When asked to respond to the fact that she has been described as 'bossy and demanding', she replied that those words would never be applied to a man.

She went on to explain her viewpoint further:

- A man is commanding, a woman is demanding
- A man is forceful, a woman is pushy
- He's assertive, she's aggressive
- He strategises, she manipulates
- He shows leadership, she's controlling
- He's committed, she's obsessed
- He's persevering, she's relentless
- A man is a perfectionist, a woman is a pain in the ass.

You might want to try using Barbra's words to start a discussion. My experience is that more men than women think it way overstates the case. More women than men think it is, well, just a succinct statement of the way things are. They identify with it deeply, as it reflects much of their experience every day.

It is well worth restating former Australian Prime Minister (PM) Julia Gillard's carefully shaped words on the evening she handed the PM role back to the previous PM, Kevin Rudd:

> 'I want to just say a few remarks about being the first woman to serve in this position. There's been a lot of analysis about the so-called gender wars, and me playing the so-called gender card, because heavens knows no-one noticed I was a woman until I raised it; but against that background, I do want to say about all of these issues, the reaction to being the first female Prime Minister does not explain everything about my prime ministership, nor does it explain nothing about my prime ministership.'

We all suffer from unconscious bias in some way and perspectives like those of Barbra Streisand and Julia Gillard help both women and men to view situations through other lenses. Just think about it next time you are looking at a female colleague's behaviour, or when you are discussing potential for career advancement. Take a little time to check yourself—that your instinctive reaction is not a case of unconscious bias. This applies to how many women view other women, as well as how men interpret women's behaviours quite differently from the same behaviour in men.

Take the time to ponder the need that each of us has to remove these filters.

Women need to claim and articulate their achievements

The third challenge is the different ways in which women and men tend to articulate and 'own' their achievements.

Over the past ten years of interviewing dozens of men and women as candidates for positions or as part of development engagements, I have consistently observed that men are generally far better than women at articulating their achievements and, in fact, sharing a coherent story about their careers.

One reason put forward in the academic literature for this is that women 'do strategy differently' and they tend to use the 'we' word much more than the 'I' word. They tend not to be as declarative, but rather consult and engage widely.

Jane Den Hollander has shared how she approached the development of her university's strategic plan as an example of a development of which she was particularly proud. She provided the entire staff with the opportunity to be part of the conversation about the strategic plan. Consequently, 'we altered it completely and changed almost everything we do'.

Seven years later ninety-two percent of staff responded to the staff survey (unprecedented in the sector) and eighty percent of staff agreed that the strategy, direction and culture of the university was the right approach, which is equally unprecedented. This was very much an open and collaborative effort.

Would Jane claim that she developed the university's strategy? Would facilitating staff engagement via such an inclusive process be seen as strong of an achievement as claiming 'I developed the strategy'? It is a real question for those who approach leading others in such a way.

In a special program we ran for mid-level female managers, mentioned in an earlier chapter, generally women were able to explain each other's contribution to the organisation much better than their own. So, over the next six to eight weeks at different sessions we built in more opportunities for them to surface and describe their achievements. In the final session they did a job interview or promotion interview role-play in groups of three—one interviewee and two interviewers.

On the whole they were good at interviewing others, but about half still needed more practice at claiming their achievements and expressing them in a way that was relevant to the role and to the interviewers.

It is important to note that the complicating factor, is strong evidence that more women than men develop strategies, policies and programs in a collaborative manner, rather than a declarative way. It is done more by working with and through a group, rather than by declaring the end goal and how the group will get there, and then trying to bring people along.

If we want women to continue to thrive, and to get the real benefits from that fifty percent of the population, we need to look at how we interact and work with one another and how we each see ourselves as leaders.

23

INCLUSION: THE KEY TO GROWTH

Know who you are as a leader

An article in *Harvard Business Review* (2013) titled 'Women Rising: The Unseen Barriers' provides a partial solution to this quiet resistance against achievement articulation.

Sometimes it is about coming to see oneself as an achiever and a leader. The authors noted: 'People become leaders by internalizing a leadership identity and developing a sense of purpose'. This is, of course, easier said than done, but naming the challenge is at least part of addressing it.

In working with a recently promoted senior female executive in another male-dominated industry, it was great to see that she had truly taken on the mantle of leadership. She had been given much broader responsibilities in the business and across the international group. She quickly came to realise that she needed a replacement for herself in her functional role and that she would have to 'let go' of a significant part of her well-developed professional expertise.

One of her responsibilities was a very high-profile and risky part of the business—and was not an area with which she was particularly familiar. When offered the (well-deserved and overdue) promotion, she was self-aware enough to stifle the first thing that came into her head, 'but I am not an expert in that field', and for that she was very proud of herself. She sought out an industry mentor to speed up her learning curve, and then quickly set about meeting the leaders of this 300-employee-strong part of the organisation.

What did she do differently from some of her peers? Over time, she had learned to describe her achievements in ways that had meaning to her male colleagues—describing them in strong 'business contribution' language. Yes, she occasionally suffered from others thinking her arrogant, but she was comfortable being respected, rather than necessarily liked, by all.

In the words of Sheryl Sandberg, she was willing to 'Lean In'. At the same time, she did not feel the need to be 'one of the boys' though she was always the sole woman at senior executive meetings and most off-sites. (Sheryl Sandberg's book *Lean In* [2011] is important reading for all women and men, despite some of the negative press and developments that have occurred more recently.)

Getting back to those 'deep seated reasons' for failure to claim achievements, I suspect that from a young age, she was given encouragement and told that she could do whatever she wanted to do. Some people have not been so fortunate and must learn how to articulate and claim their achievements. It is worth the effort!

The issues outlined above are exacerbated of course for lesbian, gay, bisexual, and transgender (LGBT+) executives, managers and employees. Where we think discrimination is much less today, the perspective of an LGBT+ would likely be quite different. The ability to be truly valued and respected for who you are from a young age can be critical to how we then lead ourselves with self-confidence as well as the affirmation of others.

Be alert to cultural differences

It takes constant effort to ensure that 'airtime' is shared equally, or at least reasonably, amongst the team members of a diverse workforce.

At MBS our students came from many different cultural backgrounds. It required a constant effort to engage those students in class who might not naturally feel inclined to speak up and contribute. It meant sometimes breaking into smaller groups, so people were comfortable enough to share their thoughts and experiences.

In the workplace the same situation often applies. In relation to personalities, there are extroverts who tend to speak, then think, then speak again; and then there are those who are more introverted who don't do their thinking out loud. They tend to think, then speak, then think again. Some people are naturally quiet and perhaps seen as non-contributors to team discussions. It's all a matter of how we design our team sessions. That's where good coaching and coaxing can come in, making sure expectations are clear, but at the same time facilitating a discussion so that each person has 'airtime'.

I have spent a considerable part of my professional career working as an executive and consultant in many countries and cultures. I always do my homework, and hope that I am respectful of the culture in which I am working. As a tall white woman, I do tend to stand out in some countries, so a good dose of humility is usually in order.

Taking the trouble to gain some good facilitation skills is very useful. There are many simple group techniques that can make a big difference to how we lead teams and workshops, and how we are then able to engage those around the table or in the room.

Another challenge that I have is that I am linguistically inept, and despite my best efforts (and part-French heritage), even simple attempts to greet people in their language have resulted in embarrassment.

One time I was opening an executive conference in Germany and tried a few words in German. One of the clients I had worked with came up to me and suggested that I don't bother to try as whatever I ended up saying, or what they heard, was not quite what I meant to say.

Use coaching and mentoring thoughtfully

You can make a difference to your teams and individuals by understanding and utilsing good coaching and mentoring. The terms often get confused. While others have different definitions, the ones I have used below work for us.

Coaching is about getting help to focus on specific attributes or role and work-related outcomes you want to achieve. An executive coach or executive advisor should understand the context of your job and organisation, and work with you on improving specific capability areas and your performance. Coaching should be well-targeted and often has an agreed timeframe. The coach is a trained and experienced professional whom you or your organisation has paid for their services.

Mentoring, on the other hand, is about being engaged with others from whom you can learn or who might take a long-term interest in your career and progress. Sometimes you might only realise after the event that a person has been a mentor to you.

A mentor is usually a higher level professional or executive who has had experiences relevant to the role of the team member being mentored. This can happen both formally and informally. The mentor might be a member of your organisation but often in a different part of the organisation, not your direct supervisor, or they might be external to your organisation. They might have had some similarities in background to you but be at a different stage of development. Generally, they are not paid for their services, but do this as part of their professional commitment and desire to see others grow and progress.

Coaching in practice

One of the challenges of coaching in practice is that too often we come across people who profess to be coaches, but their experience and understanding of their client's context could at best be described as very, very limited.

In looking for a good coach, personal and professional maturity is critical. The ability to really understand a senior manager or executive's context is pivotal. A coach does not have to have been in the role for which they are a coach, but it is usually important that they have been in roles of similar complexity and demands. They need to have had the breadth and depth to have insights into the reality of their client's experience, and it is hard to do that if you don't have some good work and life experience. A coach needs to really prod, cajole and challenge their executive clients, to get them to understand their own behaviour and values, their impact on others, and work with them through difficult and daily challenges.

My preferred term today is 'Executive Advisor' for those situations where we have worked through a leadership capability and development needs process with an individual and they, or their organisation, want to continue with a level of individual professional and executive support.

Mentoring is a professional responsibility we owe to others

Who and how have you mentored?

When we work through the development needs of professionals and we ask this, we often get some interesting responses. Some people think that it is something they will do later. Others have been part of formal mentoring programs with more or less success. We see it as an important part of professional and personal development to be available as a mentor to others. If we take the time to reflect, we can each think of people who have mentored us in our careers. In my case it goes a long way back and there are some great people I have thanked along the way—and some I thanked belatedly!

As mentioned earlier, the first of my five or so careers was as a high school teacher. Early into my career I found myself with too many commitments (something of a lifelong characteristic). I intended to resign so that I could complete the master's degree I had started while also caring for our firstborn, but I just could not bring myself to fill out the paperwork. The time spent with the Deputy

Principal during this decision process, and her continuing ability to check in on me, was pivotal to my career and development.

There were others early in my career who invited me to professional meetings, encouraged me to take on committee positions, take secondments to other roles, write reviews, lead a workshop or present at conferences and so on. None of these are things I thought of doing myself at the time, as I was quite consumed with work, study and parenting. However, my career would not have progressed the way it did without their generosity.

One of my early mentors was Dagmar Schmidmaier, who today is Director of the Chief Executive Women Leaders Program. We encountered each other at a professional development session and kept in touch. She gave me my first job in tertiary education—tutoring part-time while I was on maternity leave with our fourth child.

Today, we often see more 'reverse mentors'—junior professionals or 'digital natives'—who act as mentors to senior executives or the 'digital immigrants'. This can provide different types of insights into the professional drivers and motivations of early career workforce members. This reverse mentoring can also provide great insights to senior executives, into the changing priorities, needs and issues of their consumer base, as well as their junior workforce members.

Amongst the most important interactions though, is the mentoring that happens organically—being open and available to others, and embracing the queries, and dilemmas of younger professionals. Sometimes it's starting a conversation, asking someone how things are going, or seeking input through some open-ended questions, such as, 'What are some of the developments that have delighted you about this place?' or 'I'm interested to get a fresh perspective—what has surprised you about the organisation?'

24

BROADEN YOUR TALENT POOL

External insights: executive search firms

While it might seem a bit self-serving to say so, engaging with external search firms is another important aspect of tapping into external talent.

Sometimes it's about providing a brief to a search firm to ensure you broaden the range and nature of experience, backgrounds and talents in your teams. Executive search firms are an integral part of how smart organisations find the executive and senior management talent that they need. They can provide a level of objectivity and insight that is sometimes hard to do from inside an organisation. They also enable candidates to be drawn from the whole potential candidate pool, rather than those just looking for a job at a point in time. Executive search also involves a level of 'advocacy' for the client and thus a further point of external input.

Amongst the most frequently asked questions we address are 'What do search firms actually do?' and 'How do they do it?' Their role in the talent acquisition and development process often seems shrouded in mystery—as if they do their work through a 'black box'. This was partly the way it seemed to me too before I became a head hunter and started assisting clients with their talent acquisition challenges.

It's useful for any executive and manager to understand the nuances of recruitment and search services and how they work. Apart from seeking the best talent available for your organisation, you might find yourself in a situation where you want to be noticed.

In a personal sense too, it's helpful to understand the market you are in, the scale of typical organisations and appointments and how your experience compares.

Know the recruitment and search landscape

While many corporate and other large organisations undertake their own recruitment, most, at some stage, use a recruitment or search firm. There are three types of recruitment and search firms, which tend to relate roughly to levels in the workforce.

Contingent recruitment firms

Contingent recruitment firms operate at the entry to middle levels. They work on a fee for a placement basis. This is often where 'bulk recruitment' takes place—where a recruitment firm agrees to provide a certain number of qualified people for particular roles each month or year. These firms will be heavily driven by their own databases.

Retingent recruitment firms

Retingent recruitment firms generally operate at the middle levels where positions are mostly advertised, although some retingent recruitment firms might also proactively identify candidates. They too are paid when a candidate is placed.

Retained executive search

Retained executive search firms operate at the more senior levels, or where there are specialist skills that are hard to locate, or a deeper level of confidentiality is required.

Clients such as CEOs, Boards, heads of government agencies or businesses, and other executives, contract with an executive search firm to conduct a proactive search for a particular position. As with recruitment agencies, search firms draw on their own databases and, again depending on the nature of the role, possibly use social media sources such as LinkedIn.

But they also do original research, map the field in terms of other relevant organisations and sources for candidates, and proactively reach out to potential candidates who are not looking to change from their current roles. They will generally have good networks in the spheres in which they operate, be they particular industries, government or community organisations.

The 'retained' description refers to the fact that search firms work for an initial 'retainer' or agreed fee to start the search.

Search fees are usually paid in three instalments: the first on being commissioned to undertake a search, the second about thirty days later or when an agreed shortlist is provided to the client, and the final payment when the preferred candidate signs to accept the offered position.

Searches are usually commissioned on an exclusive basis, where one search firm is awarded the work for a particular role.

All types of organisations use search firms for senior or specialist roles. Apart from some roles in the public sector, most senior roles are not advertised.

Use search firms to provide access to a richer, well assessed candidate pool

Using a retained executive search firm means that an organisation can access a much larger candidate pool, rather than just those who might be looking for a new job or who might have noticed an ad while having their morning coffee on a Saturday.

One caveat, though, is that the very large search firms work with many organisations in the same industry. As such, they may have 'off limits' agreements—they cannot access candidates in their client companies, meaning that they cannot access the full candidate pool.

The essence of the search process by a retained executive search firm is to identify and qualify people who could do the job well but are likely not currently looking for a job and who are comfortable with where they are now.

Good search firms will complete a thorough behavioural assessment on candidates who could be considered for shortlisting. The search firm's goal is to identify and access what might be a quite specific candidate pool and to minimise the client's risk in the process. And, to clarify another sometimes-contentious issue, good search firms automatically include any potential internal candidates as part of the process. Thus, searches often need to be done with a great degree of discretion. It's important to realise that over seventy percent of the people placed with the involvement of search firms are not actually looking for a new job.

Traditionally search firms have been focused on 'C' level executives, such as CEOs and a level or two below that in large organisation, as well as Board positions. In a large organisation, the search organisation might be used for levels below that for a combination of reasons. This can include the scarcity of, and competitiveness for, good talent or the emergence of new and different types of positions. Or it can sometimes be because firms do not want to 'telescope' their business moves by more openly identifying the type of talent they are seeking.

We recently completed several searches in this category where commercial organisations were looking to build specific digital products, services and cyber security capabilities. The confidential nature of the search meant that competitors were not alerted to the client's desire to move more aggressively into this area.

A considerable part of the search firm's role includes advocacy for the client to those potential candidates—what the merits of working for that client are, or why a $70-100k drop in salary would be a great idea given you'll be able to work in the public sector or for a not-for-profit organisation where you can really make an impact.

Think broadly about diversity and diverse teams

We know that diversity in teams and organisations leads to a higher level of creativity and innovation—attributes that are now critical to help navigate uncertainty and ambiguity.

So, when thinking about the composition of your teams, it helps to think broadly. Yes, gender is one aspect, but there are many others to do with life experiences, how we think, age cohort, religion, ethnicity, and family backgrounds to mention a few.

Think about the level of diversity in both the team you lead and the team of which you are a part. How different from you are your colleagues? To what extent might a few of you be more dominant? Do you engage in groupthink? Amongst your team members do you have those who can and do challenge you and your assumptions? Do you challenge others?

You need to carefully gather the talent you need, and sometimes refresh and renew, so that you can deliver on your accountabilities, or make a success of what you are trying to do. This is not as easy as it sounds as most of us like to work with people like ourselves.

We all have biases and blind spots. They are part of how we were shaped and who we are. We need to be upfront about knowing and addressing our blind spots. It helps to make sure we are not recruiting those with whom we are immediately comfortable, who share similar backgrounds and think like us.

Broadening the talent pool can be challenging, but you need to support those who might bring different perspectives to your team and continue to value those different perspectives.

LEARNINGS AND REFLECTIONS: PART 2

Learnings about leading others with resolve

- Leading organisations through disruption is difficult and leading them from digital disruption to digital transformation is not for the faint-hearted. However, it is the new normal and requires some changes in how we lead.

- As leaders, we need to provide context for those we lead and accept that a significant part of our role is 'sense making' for others. This is a learned skill.

- Sharing information as soon as it's available, and not sitting on bad news, demonstrates a good level of transparency and helps build trust which is critical for effective leaders.

- The ability to respond quickly, particularly in a more networked environment, requires agility— the combination of speed and flexibility. Critical foundations for that agility are the capacity to trust and be trusted, and the ability to create effective teams.

- Building trust is critical in leading others through volatile times and the bedrock of effective teams.

- Trust is much more than a social virtue. Trust has economic value in that it is an asset that reduces our interaction time and our transaction costs. Mistrust can double the cost of doing business.

- Trust is about character (intent plus integrity) and competence (capabilities plus results). Trust is a reciprocal virtue—that is, we need to trust others to get trust in return.

- Our ability to trust, and be trusted by, others is part of the fabric of organisational cultures—the way we 'do things around here'.

- Self-knowledge is critical to effective leadership, and is a key ingredient in great teams. Really knowing who you are, being comfortable with that, and willing to share your vulnerability is the first step in building trust with others.

- While you need some injection of external talent from time to time, it is critical to develop and nurture the talent you have.

- As leaders we need to be able to *co-design with others*, inside and outside our organisations, to tackle issues with different perspectives.

- When employees believe they are being developed and are 'marketable' they are more likely to remain with an organisation. They don't have to leave to gain development or maintain their professional currency elsewhere.

- We all suffer from unconscious bias in some way. Take the time to ponder the need that each of us has to remove those filters.

- In looking for a good coach, personal and professional maturity is critical. The ability to really understand a senior manager's or executive's context is pivotal.

- Mentoring is an important part of your professional and personal development.

- Reverse mentoring can provide great insights to senior executives into the changing priorities, needs and issues of their citizen or consumer base, as well as their more junior workforce members.

- Be upfront about knowing and addressing your blind spots.

- You have to get outside your four walls. It's about getting engaged with your profession and the community and you don't know where it will take you. It also gives you the experience of working with difficult people.

- We build resilience through hardship. It's how you learn that even if things look impossible today, the sun will still come up tomorrow. Deal with what is in front of you and learn how to reframe.

Reflections

- Who's the best boss you have every had? What's the best peer team you have ever been part of?

- What do you think is the gap between the values your organisation espouses, and the ones that you experience? What do your peers and team members think? What can you do about that?

- If you take a secondment elsewhere for, say, twelve to eighteen months, who is ready to do your job? Who is it, on your team, that is on track for a more senior role? How many internal candidates will there be if your company asks for expressions of interest in your role, and what will be the risk or trade-off with each person?

- How would you describe the attributes of the team of which you are a member, that is a peer member, not the team you lead? Would you use words like 'effective, cohesive, supportive and committed'? Or would descriptions like 'lacking in trust', 'not really a team or truly collaborative' and 'engaging in conflict avoidance' be more appropriate?

- If we asked the same question of the team *you* lead, how would *your* team members describe their experiences as a member of your team?

- In your organisation what level of agreement and shared understanding is there about the key capabilities executives and managers need for your future organisation's success?

- Who have you mentored and how have you mentored them?

- What is your learning orientation? Where is evidence of your learning progression and your career track record?

- What is your managerial capability? How do you make decisions and deliver value to your organisations or clients? How do you deal with ambiguity and uncertainty, with complex problems?

- What is your leadership capability? To what extent do you readily accept accountability? Can you vary your communication to suit the individual or group you are with? Are you mature and self-aware and do you really understand your impact on others?

- How diverse is your team?

- How focused are you on ensuring good succession for yourself amongst your team members, and insisting that they too take succession seriously?

PART 3

LEAD WITH INSIGHTS
FROM OTHERS

We each have much to learn from others and the third part of the book brings together the learnings and insights from over twenty female executives and managers. They share their 'lessons learned' about developing their passion and purpose, getting outside their comfort zones, following their dreams and how they have dealt with personal and professional frustrations.

25

TAP IN: ADVICE FROM EXPERIENCED PROFESSIONALS

Lessons learned!

I have the privilege of working every day with women and men with all sorts of personal and professional responsibilities.

Some are board members or top-level executives leading large organisations, and others are mid-career professionals figuring out what really matters to them. Some are considering if the opportunity I am discussing with them fits with their aspirations, their experience and their values. All are trying to create the best leadership team that they can.

Through all of this, I have met many inspiring people, some names you may recognise and some which only a smaller professional circle may know.

In organising my thoughts and experiences and some lessons learned, I realised that so many others have experiences worth sharing. Their experiences are different from mine, and I know that each of them has something to offer each of us.

I approached more than twenty women who had diverse backgrounds and experiences and asked them to share a little about themselves, and just about all of them agreed.

In earlier chapters, Gartner's Robin Kranich stressed the importance of understanding the 'why' in what we do. Disney's Alisa Bowen referred to how she realised that she needed to think of her career as a marathon, not a sprint and that theme was echoed in many responses. Jody Evans shared her journey as a single parent, always taking the time to explain to her son what she needed to do and why, and involving him as much as possible.

In the next few chapters we share more of these types of experiences, of career and personal choices, risks and challenges, the passions that drove them, how they built resilience, who helped them on the journey and how they managed different types of responsibilities.

The contributors mentioned and their current roles are listed in the final pages of this book.

Career choice is as important as career progression. Go where you can change the system

Sherene Devanesen

Sherene could not figure out why I asked for her input because she stressed to me that she is 'really ordinary'. To me, Sherene is quite extraordinary. Today she is the CEO of the large disability services organisation, Yooralla, a role she took on when it was in the midst of a major crisis. She is also Chair of the Victorian Eye and Ear Hospital. Prior to that she played a key role in the strategic development and delivery of public health services from India, to Alice Springs and Darwin and in Melbourne.

Her career choices have been quite deliberate, based on her personal values and strong desire to 'value add' in whatever role she takes on. In her view, career choice is as important as career progression. Her experience is that women are more likely to change the system rather than just complain about it and this has been a hallmark of her leadership roles.

Sherene started her career in India as a medical student and she came to the Northern Territory to see how a developed country was dealing with difficult issues—only to find that Australia was not dealing well with this at all. She returned and spent ten years in Alice Springs, and then time in Darwin, before moving south to Melbourne.

Initially her career experience was not valued in Melbourne and she came to the view that she had to be two or three times as good as anyone else to be considered for the next role.

Eventually she was appointed CEO of Peninsula Health Services in outer Melbourne where she led a major turnaround. In her ten years there, the health service went from a 200-bed community hospital, to a comprehensive, award-winning health service that gained 'teaching hospital' status. She has also been very heavily involved in professional engagement and other developments sharing her time and talents. This has given her a great network to call on when she, or her organisation, needs some assistance.

Sherene's approach to any role is to focus first on getting the basics right in terms of the organisation, its strategy and financials, and, when sustainable, do the 'value add'.

This takes time, so she tended to stay seven to ten years in most roles. That has enabled her to really impact and change the system of which her organisation is a part.

Take on a major financial, governance and cultural transformation

Elizabeth Proust

Elizabeth has been chair of the Australian Institute of Company Directors, a company director and board chair of major listed, private, and not-for-profit boards for over fifteen years. In her earlier career she moved between the public and private sectors, but it was the public sector roles that involved taking on significant risks and challenges.

Elizabeth was Secretary (CEO) of the Victorian Attorney-General's Department at the age of thirty-seven, and both her age, and the fact that she was the first woman to head a government department in Victoria, gave her a higher profile than any of her predecessors.

She later became the CEO for City of Melbourne. It was in

financial difficulties, with dire politics and dysfunctional work practices. The role was very much under the spotlight. The Councillors wanted the financial problems dealt with, but many were unsupportive of the solutions. Some of their responses (publicly and privately) were negative and occasionally vitriolic. Change was made possible by a supportive management team, public backing from some Councillors, and strong support from the media.

Elizabeth's time at the City of Melbourne built early resilience, which has endured. Alongside this, there was not only a return to financial viability, there was also significant reform of Council governance, and the beginning of the revival of Melbourne as a great place to live, invest and work. It also provided her with enduring networks in many different areas, which became an important part of her later career.

Follow your dream, build a new business, rebuild to take it global

Alison Hardacre

The global health technology entrepreneur, Alison Hardacre, never wanted to be an entrepreneur. When her friends took the entrepreneurship subject in her MBA, she was not interested. At that time, she believed the word entrepreneur had a dodgy air and negative connotations. But with hindsight, she realised much of the work she did was about making a genuine difference, which is the essence of being an entrepreneur.

She was a serial improver, regardless of whether she was working in the community or corporate sectors. Her focus was regularly on system-wide improvement and seeing the opportunity to make something better. Post MBA, she landed a good role with a large health insurer and then a major bank, but she quickly realised that she would prefer to run her own business. At that stage, she did not know what business that might be so she spent time reading the financial and markets news, and after three years the 'big idea' came to her.

It was not about spreadsheets, but more a creative process that focused on what she was passionate about. That idea became HealthKit, a global health technology platform for private practitioners and their patients. It combines the functions of patient records, medical billing and accounting software and it now operates in over fifty countries.

A critical inflection point for Alison came six years ago when discussions with an investor and other stakeholders made her realise that there was a global opportunity: they could make healthcare better everywhere, particularly as the health sector is one of the last industries to digitise.

But to take on the global health market, she and her co-founder would have to rebuild all of their software from scratch, and completely change their sales model, pricing and service. It would mean massive risk and leaving the comfort of what they'd built behind, but it would also be a shot at building a 'unicorn' (a billion-dollar business).

They chose the unicorn. It took twelve months to build the platform and the new sales, service and pricing model, and in the ensuing years they have dealt with many different issues. Looking back, they believe that going global was absolutely the right decision, but it was tough.

Alison regularly assists other budding entrepreneurs, and, as she notes, 'So many people have a fantasy about running their own business and so many regret that they don't do it. If you do want to grow your own business, just do it. The key is action, always action—ask yourself 'What can I do today to build my business?' and then prioritise around that; everything else is distraction.'

Get engaged with your professional community. Who knows where it will lead?

Kate Carnell

Kate has had a significant career in business and politics, and she is now Australia's Small Business and Family Enterprise Ombudsman.

She started her career as a community pharmacist and then

bought her first pharmacy business, mortgaging her home in the process. There were few women owners at the time and she also became involved in the Pharmacy Guild, becoming President of the ACT. The Guild was involved in a lot of lobbying and she developed a public profile.

Alongside this, a group of local business people asked her to join them and run for political office. She declined on multiple occasions then relented due to a conversation at a rally where she spoke. A fellow business leader suggested to her that it was time to 'put up or shut up' if she really wanted to make the ACT a better place to live and run a business.

She joined the Liberal Party, stood for office, and three years later became the Chief Minister for the Australian Capital Territory. She was elected twice, which continues to be a record for a female political leader at that level in Australia.

Kate has been the 'first woman to...' in a number of situations. The essence for her was getting involved in the local community and working hard to make a difference. As she puts it, 'You have to get outside your four walls. It's about getting engaged with your profession and the community and you don't know where it will take you. It also gives you the experience of working with difficult people'. If you are going to do something, give it one-hundred percent—or don't do it!

What is the worst that can happen?

Lalitha Biddulph

Singapore-based Lalitha of J.P. Morgan believes she would not have the global leadership role she has today without some prodding when she was about twelve years into her career.

She had not applied for an Account Management role that had recently opened up. This was a level higher than her current role and she believed it did not play to her strengths. However, her boss's boss called her directly asking why she had not applied. She replied that her strengths were in delivering projects, and she did not believe she could handle the level of networking and relationship building in the Account Management role.

To this day Lalitha remembers the reply she received: 'That is exactly why you need to go for it. You are either going to learn very quickly how to influence and build relationships or you are going to fail spectacularly—either way what do you have to lose? You will learn new skills and move on to bigger roles or you will fail and return back to roles that focus on delivery'.

She went for the role and was appointed. She found it really challenging initially but it taught her how to influence others without having direct responsibility for them, to look strategically at problems, and to solve for the firm rather than a specific customer.

This role was pivotal in her shift in moving from a role that used her management ability well to the experience of real leadership and influence, which she has drawn on ever since.

Find your passion and make it your life's work

Andrea Hull

Early in her school and university years Andrea came to understand the benefits and enrichment of an actively engaged life. After starting her career as a secondary school teacher, she moved to London where she saw more closely the transformative power of the Arts and creativity.

On returning to Australia she joined the Community Arts Program of the Australia Council, thus beginning the pursuit of a lifelong passion. She felt then, and continues to believe, that an authentic and distinctive cultural life is the key to Australia's maturation.

At age thirty-nine, Andrea became the first woman to head a government department in Western Australia, the WA Department of the Arts. Her daughter was born during this time, before paid maternity leave existed, and she was the family breadwinner. Her position required long days and evening work and she notes that she did not always get the balance right.

More recently, in what she refers to 'Act 3' of her life, she has taken on further family responsibilities and believes she is now better at the blend. But she knows too that her passion applied to her CEO and Executive roles in the Cultural sector over thirty-five years, with the last nine as Board member of some iconic institutions, has had a real impact.

Nina Anderson

After graduation, Nina, founder of Anderson Advisory, landed her dream job with a highly-regarded consumer public relations company. But she quickly realised that she hated it.

She later went to work for a boutique corporate public relations firm and this experience made her career. She was given responsibility, encouragement and support, and flourished.

After working across Europe and the west coast of the US she decided she wanted to start her own business. At the time she had two young children and needed some seed funding. Her dream was receding. But then, 'I was lucky enough to be made redundant and that was it, funding granted! I was free to pursue my dream'.

She quickly learned that, 'founding a business and keeping it going builds more resilience than I ever thought I had.' After six years her business continues, providing people at all levels of business with access to professional communications support. She has continued to invest in her development and innovate, and Anderson Advisory now involves a hybrid model of artificial intelligence and consulting.

Develop a new passion, if what you want to do is not possible right now

Lucinda Nolan

Lucinda, currently CEO of the Ovarian Cancer Research Foundation, spent nearly thirty-three years in Emergency Services—thirty-two years with Victoria Police and eight months with the Country Fire Authority.

She found, once she had her three children, Victoria Police did not offer flexible work options. It was either full-time, or you resigned. She looked for positions with routine rosters, and discovered more corporate roles or functions, rather than front-line service delivery.

These opportunities, which initially felt like a punishment, gave her a breadth of knowledge and skills that she would not have experienced had she progressed via a normal police career path. This included areas she found very stimulating such as strategic and business planning, corporate support roles, intelligence management and education. It made her realise the value of horizontal progression over and above vertical progression, particularly at key management levels.

Rachel Dapiran

Rachel's early career was in the trade union movement and as a political advisor. As a senior advisor to the Premier of her state, she was fairly close to the 'centre of power' at a relatively young age.

She came to the view that this was not how she wanted to spend the rest of her life, particularly when having a family was on the horizon. She looked at the areas of her advising work that fascinated her most, and realised it was decisions around urban and regional planning.

There were many factors to consider with planning that made it appealing—social, economic, political and others. The issues were complex and important. She went back to university and completed a master's degree in urban planning.

Coming back into the part-time and then the full-time workforce meant 'flatlining' for a while, in a number of ways: she had no real experience as a planner so needed to start near the bottom with younger recent graduates, she took a considerable pay cut, and she was a long way from that 'centre of power'. It was something she had to adjust to, but she loved the work and gained relatively rapid promotion.

She is now Executive Director for Strategy, Engagement and Futures with the Victorian Planning Authority.

If you are frustrated, use it to act and bring about change

Jody Evans

Melbourne Business School's Jody Evans found that when she was restricted to a purely academic role, she was unable to use her professional and domain skills.

She had worked with not-for-profit organisations for the past fifteen years and spent much of her time helping them craft compelling and unique impact narratives. She advised cultural organisations on strategies to engage their stakeholders more effectively.

Over her years at the Business School, she believed the approach to fundraising was being undertaken at the expense of genuine relationships with members of the MBS community.

Jody realised that she could not just mutter and complain from the sidelines. She was building her career at the school and, in the end, believed she could make a difference to the organisation she cared about.

She put her thoughts together and asked for a meeting with the then Dean. He listened and her role was extended to that of Associate Dean, Engagement, leading the school's impact agenda and engaging stakeholders in shared value initiatives. She has had a great impact on how the school interacts with alumni, business and the broader community.

If your capabilities are not appreciated, move elsewhere

Susan Oliver

Susan Oliver is a board chair and non-executive director of listed, unlisted and not-for-profit entities with a focus on the built environment and innovation.

She started her career in the construction industry and was the first woman to complete that degree at the University of Melbourne in the early 1970s. She is another person whose parents did not have tertiary education but helped her to believe that she could do anything she wanted to do.

However, Susan found significant challenges, mostly gender-related, and this was frustrating. But she really wanted to make a difference. Her passion was equity and access to low cost housing, making things run better and applying innovative approaches. To do this she needed to be in positions of influence.

A major inflection point for her was joining the public sector. She rose to be an executive level manager in the then Housing Department, and later moved to the Department of Industry where she rediscovered manufacturing and technology.

Susan's early negative experiences, over time, have led to an amazing portfolio of interests and influence including board and chair roles with many listed and unlisted companies. She is also Co-Founder of Scale Investors, which has invested in twelve women-led start-up companies.

Jane Den Hollander

Jane has recently spent eight years making a demonstrable impact as Vice-Chancellor and CEO of Deakin University. She describes herself as a woman leader, a feminist, and like many women in this book, was the first in her family to achieve a university degree.

She has been in higher education all of her adult life, across three jurisdictions, in both academic and professional roles.

After immigrating to Australia with her Australian husband and their two children, she worked in a university where, over a period of four years, she rose to a position of significant profile and success.

A very senior Executive position came up and she was invited to apply. It was a public process between two internals and she was seen as a 'change agent' with 'an entrepreneurial mindset'. She did not get the job. However, about three months later the rival university offered her a similar level role and she was successful. This was the role from which she was invited to be the Vice Chancellor for Deakin University.

Her initial failure caused deep reflection on what she was good at, and not good at, and what she wanted to be and do. She decided that it was time to expand her skills and go for a bigger leadership role if it arose. She reflected that if she had not lost the first job, her experience would have been narrower and she would not have been offered the Deakin role. Was she lucky? Jane thinks that she worked very hard to achieve what she has to date but, yes, luck is an important part of any career.

Chris Gillies

Though she was dux of her year at school, with two older brothers going to university, being the girl, Chris was expected to get a job and get married. And yet, fate stepped in—through a friend of the family, she got a job with Data Control. This was BC, Before Computers, in the commercial world. It was, as she puts it, 'when the Melbourne University computer still had valves'.

That early start in with Data Control did not continue. She needed more flexibility: married at nineteen with two daughters by the age of twenty-two, Chris worked a number of jobs—laboratory assistant, medical records clerk and programmer—before finally taking a role at Xavier College. She stayed for nine years eventually becoming assistant bursar, and as Chris puts it, 'I think I grew up at Xavier College'.

When her children were old enough, Chris left her comfort zone to get back into the commercial world. This meant taking a few steps down to become a business systems analyst for a company introducing leading-edge technology into banks.

After six months she was asked to run a division with over fifty people and realised that some people had a far better opinion of her capabilities than she did herself. This caused some reflection. She realised that the minute she was put in charge of people and responsible for their success, she became a leader and successful leadership comes from having the right people around you.

As Chris was in on the ground floor of the IT industry, this soon enabled her to have significant roles with major IT consulting firms. These roles included leading transformations, managing mergers and acquisitions, and, later, sitting on listed, government and NFP Boards.

As her career has required the challenging combination of technical nous, people and culture leadership, and strong business savvy, Chris has written a Career Snapshot titled *A Fortunate Life: Some thoughts on how to recognise opportunities and take them.*

Somewhere along the line someone else believed in and prodded you

For many of the women mentioned in this chapter, there was one special person who helped them along the way, who had given them real encouragement and supported them.

This might have been their life partner who had great belief and who co-parented well, took time out, was there for the setbacks, or was otherwise truly present for support. Or it might have been one or more bosses who gave them particular encouragement or saw something in them that they did not necessarily see themselves.

Alisa Bowen

Alisa had a series of great bosses who believed in her and gave her good exposure and that level of backing made all the difference.

Her observation was that mostly those men had been self-assured and secure in their own values and integrity, and their talent development successes had been a source of personal pride.

They were thus great sponsors, who built a sense of mutual trust and loyalty. The worst sponsors are those who engage because it ticks some kind of corporate box of executive duties.

Lalitha Biddulph

Lalitha had a career-shaping experience with her first senior female boss Judy. Judy was a personable single mother and her desk and office were full of pictures of her daughter. She often shared personal anecdotes and compared parenting with some of the issues the team was dealing with at work.

The big lesson for Lalitha was the importance of bringing her whole authentic self to work. Somewhere along the way, she had developed the notion that she needed to uphold a separate 'work persona'. Her work colleagues did not know anything about Lalitha the person. By example, Judy showed how to balance the personal and the professional. It was not a sign of weakness to show personal traits that make one more human.

It changed Lalitha's way of working so that her staff and colleagues opened up about their personal issues, which allowed the team to plan and handle any situations that came up that might have otherwise impacted work. It created a supportive work environment, with the leadership team watching out for each other.

Abigail Bradshaw

For Abigail, contrary to media reporting and public discourse, it was some great men in uniform, in particular, three Naval admirals.

One taught her the critical nexus between good governance and managing operational risk, another how to plan and the third gave her 'enough rope to hang myself, but always pulled me into the safety net until I didn't need it anymore'.

All of them had a level of confidence in her capability, which exceeded her own assessment. All of them actively encouraged and assisted her to find opportunities outside the Navy where they convinced her she would thrive.

Sherene Devanesen

Amongst those who supported Sherene's career were two Secretaries/CEOs and Deputy Secretary of her state's Department of Health. They saw her potential early on and promoted her by way of inviting her to join state-wide committees and to undertake reviews.

At Peninsula Health she had a supportive Board chair over ten years, without whose full backing, it would have been very difficult to progress major organisational changes.

Early on she found the community of Alice Springs supportive, and this enabled her to further develop Aboriginal Medical Services working with local communities.

Kathryn Fagg

Kathryn found that going to work for a large multinational company with a strong graduate program provided exceptional and robust training early on. Moving to McKinsey enabled her to gain breadth across sectors and build the confidence that she could go almost anywhere and take on different issues.

But the key to success was learning to work closely with the people in the organisations with whom she was consulting. It also meant that, over time, she came to the view that she wanted to run a business. Having done that now in a number of organisations, what makes her really proud is that she has improved how those organisations work and made them more successful. She has helped others develop and seeing others thrive is very satisfying.

Jody Evans

Sometimes it is other family members who provide great support. For Jody the person who has had the biggest influence on her career has been her sister, who is also an academic and they have provided great mutual support for each other. As Jody describes it:

> Academia can be a brutal sector, 'publish or perish' is alive and well. My sister is my co-author, research partner, strategic advisor and greatest advocate. We have carried each other during periods of maternity leave and kept each other publishing. We have worked together to secure major research grants and shared them between our respective institutions. My sister is the person I am most honest with about my successes and my failures. Most importantly we have helped each other juggle parenting and careers. Our kids go to the same school and we coordinate calendars for school drop off and pickups.

Asa Lautenberg

Asa is Director of Human Resources and Services at the German manufacturing company Samson, a role she has had for the past eight months.

This was a big shift from the airline Lufthansa where, along with three years at the airline technology company Amadeus, she had spent most of her previous seventeen-year professional career.

She had many opportunities and a whole range of different bosses in the aviation industry. But, in the end, she gave up that high-profile opportunity (along with its cheap travel for the family) to join a mid-sized privately-owned manufacturing company.

She surprised herself with her choice as she had another offer with a firm that would have been more prestigious. Asa's choice came down to one of her values and beliefs. In the process of selection for her current role, she immediately saw the CEO, some of her future peer colleagues, and some of the board members of Samson as real mentors for her.

She has had a steep learning curve but is enjoying a boss and group of peers she really trusts, and her peers are also great sparring partners.

Resilience is built through difficult decisions and seeing things through

Kate Carnell

Kate found that her time in politics was both exhilarating and fulfilling. She developed resilience through developing a 'thick skin' and 'putting things in boxes' so that they did not impact her personally. 'It is important not to take criticism personally and don't dwell on things you can't change.'

Her view is that if you get the opportunity to make a real difference, take it. It will come with significant personal and professional challenges—but you won't regret having a go!

Asa Lautenberg

Before starting her professional career, Asa fell pregnant during her university course. She took a year off, later enrolled in her master's degree and had a year with each of her two children at home. She put herself forward for an internship at Lufthansa Cargo and in the end was offered and took a three-month appointment.

It was tough, not just with the family responsibilities, but it was also very much a 'man's world' at the company. She learned to deal with organisational politics but did not enjoy it. Over the years though, it did help her clarify the sort of environment in which she really did want to work and contribute.

She had to learn resilience early and found it difficult at first as in her view, 'women often take things very seriously, and it is not just a job to us, and we need to learn to filter out what is not helpful'. She learned that ability to filter out and make sure she did not let things get her down. Physical workouts at the gym became important times to set aside.

Alison Hardacre

For entrepreneur Alison Hardacre, capital raising has definitely built her resilience.

She successfully raised $1.6 million in equity after speaking to 134 investors. She is comfortable pitching and noted investors regularly compliment her on her pitching skills.

She believes that things have improved significantly over the past six years for women entrepreneurs but they continue to have to prove more than others. Despite this, together with her business partner Lachlan, Alison has grown a team from scratch and grown a business in fifty different countries, with $4.5 million outside investment, allowing her business to became operational much earlier than is the norm. It also allowed her and Lachlan to hold more equity than other comparable organisations.

Elisabet Wreme

Elisabet believes that the earlier you can develop resilience through hardship, in your career, the better it will be for you. She says, 'It is the way you learn that even if things look impossible today, the sun will still come up tomorrow. Deal with what is in front of you and learn how to reframe.'

She had the good fortune of having a person who worked for her who turned out to be a master of reframing: 'You could tell when he got stressed, he always walked back and forth with the mobile glued to his ear. Then, he would come back the next day with a very different mindset, enabling him to resolve nearly anything that was thrown at him.'

She learned so much from one of her team, highlighting that you can learn from anyone, it doesn't have to be your manager or mentor.

Glenys Beauchamp

Glenys has worked on some of the 'big ethical questions that tug at your role as a public servant and impact a whole lot of people'.

While she now heads the Australian federal government's Health Department, in her earlier career at state/territory level she was in a policy role for just four months when a Board of Inquiry was held into deaths in a home for people with disabilities.

She had to take the stand for many days, but there was a negative outcome for her department. She then had to shoulder accountability for all of those developments leading up to the enquiry, despite it all happening before her time.

She believes she was fortunate because the Chief Minister at the time came out in the press and strongly supported her. He then appointed her the deputy of a new government agency to fix the problems identified in the Board's report. It was a challenging time for her, personally and professionally, and she had to 'toughen up and build coping strategies', which she did.

She believes, too, that she learned a lot about how to shape policies with a strong operational understanding of the implications on the ground, the legal framework and the range of capabilities that need to be put in place to achieve the required outcome. It required a holistic approach and a strong grasp of all the 'moving parts'. She describes that as looking for the 'unintended consequences' (which a friend of mine refers to as the unlooked for consequences).

Susan Oliver

As outlined earlier, Susan's love of things technical has taken her into many traditional male-dominated areas. When she walked into that first all-male lecture room as an undergraduate, the lecturer promptly told the class that women belonged to the kitchen or the bedroom.

She has been bullied on building sites and threatened with concrete shoes on the bottom of the Yarra River. She has built projects and teams and had them taken over by the preferred male, made breakthroughs in thinking and then men in the team got together and formed a consulting practice around that concept. But she has built great resilience but, 'I no longer take it on the chin. I punch back.'

Keep your integrity

Elisabet Wreme

For Elisabet, integrity has always been very important. She expects to feel pride in the organisation she is working for. Whenever possible she has tried to select a job with a manager that she can respect. Throughout different parts of her career, she has had to bring many difficult issues to the surface. This has never really scared her since, in the end, the most important thing is that 'you can live with yourself'.

Elisabet's advice is to always choose your organisation and manager well, and if possible, don't put yourself in a financial position that takes makes you feel trapped. It has served her well. Enormous freedom and courage come from that feeling of having options.

Jane Sherlock

Jane is Chief People Officer of the infrastructure company John Holland. This is an industry where she has spent the past eight years as well as early in her career.

She developed resilience early on when she had to deal with the 'old boys club' who tried to impose antiquated ideas on what a woman's role should be. The tables were turned more recently in her role at CPB Contractors (formerly Leighton Contractors) where her portfolio included Safety, Health, Environment and Quality, ICT and Corporate Affairs. This is a large remit on its own in the construction business, let alone alongside all the People (HR & IR) functions she held simultaneously.

Today Jane is an executive leader in the infrastructure sector with what she calls a 'strategic implementation' mindset and a great reservoir of passion for her work. She has worked with three CEOs who have not only sponsored her progress, but with whom she has worked collaboratively in strong professional partnerships to address difficult strategic issues.

At different times though, she has experienced conflicting values with parent companies and this has required a high level of personal resilience and integrity to manage.

Ultimately, Jane left those organisations, even if she did not have another role lined up. She wants to continue to be a role model for her sons, which along with the development of strong teams, she regards as major career achievements.

'If it doesn't feel right ...'

One of our contributors noted that the word 'integrity' is always listed on expected corporate behaviours or core values. It gets printed on mouse mats, screen savers and it's everywhere to remind employees that integrity is a core value.

In previous roles though, her integrity has been severely challenged, and in the end, she departed those roles after making no headway with those to whom she reported, 'In my working career I have been asked to:

- Sign contracts and not question the value to the firm.

- Sign off on contracts where the product we were buying was not yet built.

- Route purchases through a certain supplier often unnecessarily so they can 'add value'.

- Hire staff though specific agencies that have close relationships with certain people in the firm.

- Send staff to training courses where the training firm has strong links with people in the firm.

- Use consulting firms, where ex-senior employees of the firm work, to endorse decisions we already worked through.

- Sign off on expense statements for staff that 'have special privileges' for example to hold regular meetings in expensive restaurants.'

She has taken the approach that if it does not feel right, she questions it, and raises it through all the channels till she has a satisfactory response.

She has refused to endorse or have anything to do with what does not feel right. In many situations this gets resolved but there are many times when raising it has not been the best career choice. She has been told to 'stop being difficult' and 'just go with the flow'. Once it was, 'You don't understand our culture, this is how it works here'. Then there was the time she was told, 'Don't question it, it's the Captain's pick and he is allowed that'.

She resigned from one role when she could no longer sleep at night because of some of the decisions she was being asked to endorse. She still remembers what another executive said to her when she told him she had resigned: 'Good on you, you are leaving with your integrity intact and you can hold your head high'.

She had to ask herself why he was in that role if he was happy to look the other way as she kept raising issue, upon issue. She took her 'difficult' self to another organisation where her integrity was valued.

Lucinda Nolan

Lucinda knows better than most that Emergency Services can be a tough field to work in. Her role as CEO of her state's Country Fire Authority (CFA) was probably one of her toughest, with very challenging times, which were difficult to navigate. (The issues with the CFA's proposed Enterprise Bargaining Agreement are a matter of public record.)

The clear lesson for Lucinda was that if you take on such a key leadership role, then you need to ensure that decisions you make are in the best interests of the community and the organisation you serve, 'If you don't stand up for these principles, then you stand for nothing. Sometimes the decisions you make aren't the toughest thing you have to do, it is living with the repercussions that proves most difficult'.

The Minister responsible for the CFA resigned from the government's cabinet the week prior. When the government sacked the board, Lucinda resigned as CEO two hours later. She knew that it would be difficult re-enter the public sector, to which she had dedicated her working life. Today, Lucinda is CEO of the Ovarian Cancer Research Foundation.

Carer responsibilities help us to balance insights and blend experiences

In taking in some of the comments below about managing carer responsibilities, it is helpful to understand the context for many of 'baby boomers' that are often not fully realised by those who think we might have 'had it easy'. In fact, it was only a few years before I started my career that women no longer had to give up work when they married.

There was also no HECS and university was not 'free' early on. In my time, most of us needed to work very hard to get a scholarship to attend university, and then support ourselves through part-time work. In many cases too those scholarships came with being 'bonded' to an employer for five years or so, which had both pros and cons.

There was very little if any form of maternity leave (let alone paid leave), and no one had ever heard of paternity leave. The only paternity leave Robert ever took was half a day to drive me and the latest baby home from hospital, and that was the norm.

Childcare and early learning centres were rare and largely unregulated, and there were certainly no such things as 'child care benefits'. You paid for all of it.

It took quite a while to save up the deposit for a home, as you needed at least a twenty-five percent deposit, and the mortgage then attracted bank interest rates up to eighteen percent in the 1980s.

Travel was much more expensive and took longer, and mobility was more difficult.

We have progressed quite some way since, though it often feels like two steps forward and one step back.

Kate Carnell

Kate learned early on that you can't be all things to all people all the time. Superwoman does not exist. In her industry roles and political life, she took the view that she did not do breakfast events (usually), so that she could take her children to school, but was (usually) not home for dinner.

If she was home in the evening then that was a bonus. She and her husband, a senior public servant, worked out what was possible for them. Her advice is to discuss it, make those decisions, be clear about what is possible and then just get on with it. It was also important to get the help you need—housework, ironing and childcare. It is important to plan quality family time and not let work get in the way.

Lucinda Nolan

Lucinda is the mother of three children, and her eldest son is on the autism spectrum. As she explains, 'Anyone living with autism will tell you, it is no picnic—but the strength of character and resilience of all my children makes me a very proud mother. Family and children have always come first and I am able to say that my husband and I have no regrets around our working lives and our priorities. It was always the children first'.

Rachel Dapiran

Along with Lucinda, one of the children of Rachel and her partner is also on the autism spectrum and that requires particular arrangements and sensitivities. Her advice is to ask others for help and provide help to others. Build a good network, meet and make friends with the other parents and teachers so they know your situation and that of your children. Be happy with getting the balance between work and home right eighty percent of the time.

Jane Sherlock

Jane sought out flexible arrangements early on. She encourages others to get some support and recognise you can't do it all. Her partner has always been supportive of her ambitions and achievements and shares the parenting responsibilities.

Elisabet Wreme

For Elisabet and her partner, it was hard since they didn't have any support from grandparents and they both worked. So they learned to share the load. Her husband went to work really early and she did the drop offs. She often had to work late, so he did the pick-ups. They planned their work travel to ensure they weren't travelling at the same time etc. Elisabet makes a good point in noting that they were lucky that they had kids who rarely got sick, so it all worked out, but it was touch and go many times. Her advice is if you can afford it, don't hesitate to get help, such as a cleaner. That way you can spend any free time with the kids or on yourself.

Nina Anderson

Nina recalls that even though it was only ten years ago, she didn't qualify for paid maternity leave the first time around (by three weeks). Corporate firms were less accommodating and you had to work from an office, as it was deemed unacceptable to work while you had children around you.

She had to make a choice between a corporate affairs career, which is twenty-four seven, and being around her children more. She chose the latter and did not regret it, but it was very hard when she was watching the soaring careers of her friends and peers who didn't have children then or who didn't have them at all. She notes that, 'It does balance out in the end, but at the time it's really tough to get your head around, and hard to balance your ambition with reality'.

Nina now feels like she has a really good balance. She works full-time on her own business and has control over her career. She is able to take some time over school holidays to spend with her kids and then, 'I am alive with ideas for my business. It's a good place to be.'

Giving others a helping hand enriches your experiences

Giving back in different ways tends to become more important the more secure and experienced we become. It does take time, effort and preparation, but is usually appreciated. It also establishes good role modelling for others.

Lalitha Biddulph

Lalitha takes an active role in participating in J.P. Morgan's graduate intake programs, often delivering course content at the training programs. She enjoys delivering courses on technical content alongside issues of ethics, integrity and diversity.

She also does leadership sessions and round tables with graduates a few years into the firm, and mentors some of the young staff. As she explains it: 'I am proud to think that I have influenced so many young people to think differently about their careers. Every time, I do a session with the young graduates who join our firm, I walk away from the meetings energised and excited at what lies ahead for them'.

Glenys Beauchamp

Glenys appreciates the fact she was supported by both women and men in different parts of her journey. For example, senior men such as the City Manager for Canberra, Mr John Turner, or the Secretary of the Department of Urban Services, Rod Gilmour, had a big influence on her career and character. However, it was Lisa Paul, the former Secretary of the Australian Department of Education, Employment and Workplace Relations who gave her the support and opportunity to join the Australian Public Service.

Like Glenys, before her federal government career, Lisa had worked in the ACT state /territory government. She understood the value of the strategic shaping and delivery of services at the practical and pragmatic level.

Glenys' earlier issues in ACT Government gave her a quite different perspective on different types of crises. She believes they are just part of the everyday experience of government and the volatility of political leadership.

She feels privileged to have been on the journey for major reforms in social and economic policy, including childcare, child support, and pensions, as well as establishing a new Department for Regional Australia.

In her current role as Secretary/CEO of the Department of Health for Australia, she is able to have a different level of influence. At the same time, she is known as a strong people leader and likes people to do well so quite a few of her former team members are now leaders in their own right.

Christine Kilpatrick

A former Neurologist, chair of the Committee of Chairmen of Victorian Teaching Hospitals and then Divisional Director, Christine found that working on a school board was very helpful to her development.

Develop perspective for the long-term

A common thread from many of our female interviewees is the need to develop your own perspective—for the long-term.

Lucinda Nolan

Lucinda believes life is too short to worry about whether or not to take a risk. She has gained a sense of perspective and realised she has rarely not taken up an opportunity that has presented itself. She believes that the only way to learn and grow is to take a risk, and risk failure. Failure tended to be her best teacher.

Elisabet Wreme

Elisabet found it best not to stress too much about titles and positions, 'We are all just people'. Most people also have good intentions. It sometimes just doesn't look like that because their perspectives are different but, 'If you can understand their perspective, most things can get solved'.

Lalitha Biddulph

Lalitha has come to realise that every decision we make has consequences, every decision is made at a point in time, and decisions she made changed the course of her life—sometimes subtly, sometimes many years on.

She says, 'Every decision you make has to sit right with you, with people close to you and with your values. It is your decision, not some else's opinion, that should dictate how you decide, that is the only way to explain it'.

She left home to go to school in a different city, moved countries for a career opportunity, took a six-month break when she had her first child and a three-week break when she had her second. She worked full-time while her husband was the primary carer for their children, moving countries again for her career.

All these decisions have consequences but, with the benefit of hindsight, she would not have changed them. On balance: 'I am happy with the way my life has turned out!'

Sherene Devanesen

Like Lalitha and Elisabet, Sherene changed her country base a number of times. Sherene has ten 'lessons learned' that she shares with others that exemplify her experiences, even if some of her work took time and a lot of effort to be recognised:

- Do your job well and the rest will follow
- Deliver on expectations.
- Build strong, productive relationships with all stakeholders.
- Lead by example.
- Be empathetic yet firm.
- Use a collaborative, inclusive approach to management.
- Aim for excellence.
- Be flexible, listen to others.
- Ensure personal physical, emotional and mental well-being.
- Do not move too frequently, stay until you can 'value add'.

Nina Anderson

When Nina first started her business, people used to tell her all the statistics about how many businesses fail in their first year. This used to frustrate her, but now she says, 'I just ignore them'.

At the same time, she believes it's important to never stop learning and always have an open mind. She makes a big effort to keep up her learning and meeting people who are doing different and challenging things. This has helped her to challenge the status quo, to adapt and take advantage of market changes.

She gives the warning to be 'very careful who you let near your head. There are a lot of people who will try to hold you back and bring you down with their fear and negativity,' but, 'when something feels unbearably tough, don't stop. This is when you really need to persevere with your vision and to keep going with your work. It's also usually the bottom of the change curve and you're just about to experience the magic.'

The Gillies Motto: You have control of your life, so take it

Chris Gillies believes that life is ten percent what happens to us, and ninety percent how we respond.

We have control of your life—take it! In her Career Snapshot, Chris provides some of her key life lessons:

Lesson 1: As a woman, your life is made up of many stages. You can have a family and a career, but it may not be all at the same time. You can make time! There is still a lot of life after your children grow up.

Lesson 2: Go for opportunities as they present themselves. Learn from the experience and don't be afraid to 'have a go'. Take the risk; take the lead. Just be the best at whatever you do, no matter how menial—you will be noticed. I have always worked on the principle that the only person who would ever stop me from achieving success would be me.

Lesson 3: Read the people around you, watch behaviours. They are your greatest feedback device, and most importantly—know that they are reading yours. Think about how you present, step back and have a look at you. How do you come across?

Lesson 4: It's okay to re-appraise where you're going. If it's not right, change it. Be prepared to take a step down or sideways to get where you want to go.

Lesson 5: Understand and differentiate between the things you can change and those you can't. Don't waste time focusing on those things you have absolutely no control over.

Lesson 6: You never get there on your own. Invest in your relationships and network—it will become your most valuable asset. Think about getting a mentor.

Lesson 7: A woman's life is a journey, and it's okay not to have career objectives. Flexibility is key—children and family must always come first. Learn from every job you do, see where it takes you, and just keep learning.

Lesson 8: Be generous in being available to others. Share, be flexible and allow others to learn from you.

Lesson 9: Always keep your glass at least half full—look for the positive, look for the solution, and focus on tangible outcomes. People and organisations gravitate towards positive. Be that magnet.

Lesson 10: Finally, acknowledge and own your strength as a woman. Don't undersell yourself. I love the Helen Reddy song 'I Am Woman'. When I look back on my life, my biggest achievement—my greatest happiness and success—has been from my two daughters. Without them life would be a bit empty despite the success on the work front. So, I would encourage you to develop your inner strength, know yourself, love your family, listen to your body, invest in your relationships, and have fun. And above all: have a winning, positive attitude and be the best at everything you do.

26

THINK DIFFERENTLY: YOUNG IS OKAY

The indirect path is more often than not the one we travel

The ability, and necessity, to adapt, to see life's challenges as a journey, and to have the perspective of what Jane Den Hollander calls her 'wiser, older self', is apparent in the stories and experiences of many women.

As Elizabeth Proust has pointed out, women are still disproportionately responsible for childcare and aged parents. While these responsibilities are clearly primary concerns of many of the women quoted here, we are also generally a privileged group: we are educated, in good jobs, and many of us have partners who have taken on a good share of responsibilities. Most of us have had options and made choices.

But even so, many of those journeys have not been easy. There have been some headwinds and blockages and negativity along the way, which has required a high level of determination, resilience and perseverance. It's about making choices that fit your personal values.

Like the sailing analogy, our journeys have required quite a bit of tacking, and a straight career line is not always possible or even sensible.

In the words of my daughter, Katie, 'Lead the way you want to be led while appreciating that others have a different story. You are part of someone else's story and make sure that your input into their story makes their next chapter a better one'.

This final chapter is Katie's response, as an emerging leader, to the questions asked and responses received from the other twenty women, who range from mid-career through to the most experienced of leaders.

When I was working on the latter part of this work, Katie was going through a challenging period, and was considering a number of different career options. As a thirty-something leader and manager in her profession I asked her to put down her thoughts in the same way I had asked others. Her contribution was from both her heart and head and it seemed best to share as a single communication.

The response headings are those asked of all the women approached for input.

Katie's insights so far...

Q: How would you describe yourself?

A career family person… I'm my best self, the best mum, wife, and my most productive at work, when work and family are in balance.

Q: Your first professional career?

I am a Paediatric Occupational Therapist working with kids who have developmental delays and disabilities (and also qualified as a school teacher). I love seeing the extraordinary in other's ordinary, and the myriad of steps it takes to achieve what, for some, just comes so easily.

'Think differently' is a personal and professional mantra. It helps me to support families to see the perceived insurmountable challenges that might be before them as a challenge, to think differently.

I am inspired to be innovative in my everyday practice and to think differently because the children and young people I work with deserve that, to see the possibility through the challenges and tackle set-backs with a new resolve. Sometimes the most difficult of situations can be overcome with the simplest of changes. A child won't be able to reach the tap at kinder, so use a block to stand on. A child might be picked on by other children so give the other children more credit than that, teach them the skills to engage with their new friend. Changing young mindsets will lead to a much better, more inclusive world.

Q: Name two career inflection points, roles or experiences that made a significant difference to your career progression, from a positive (or negative) perspective.

I had been an OT for about five years and had found my passion and niche in working with families who have a child with an Autism Spectrum Disorder. But I had a desire to do more, to share more.

Throw your hat in, go for it!

A few positions had been advertised but I didn't think I had the experience for them. In talking to Mum about it she said something that I've never forgotten, and remind myself of in times of doubt: 'Who do you think you are?'

I was quite taken aback and somewhat confused but then she added, 'there's a panel of people whose role is to decide whether or not you have the skills and experience, that's not for you to decide. If you want the job, you throw your hat in and see what happens!' I love that. If you want something in life, you go for it. Even if you don't get the role, you ask for feedback. When a role like that comes up again you use the feedback to ensure that gap isn't there to be noted next time.

Young is okay

I had a role as a Head of Department in a school when I was thirty-one. Every one of the staff I was leading was older than me and had been at the school in that department longer than I had. I didn't believe the department had the best people working to their potential. I felt significant changes and much higher expectations needed to be met. This was a daunting experience. I respected these people dearly and knew they were good at what they did, but I could see they had become complacent in their roles.

I worked with each of them individually to draw out their passions and remind them of why they came to work every day. We then worked together as a team to identify what it was we wanted our team to look like, be like and feel like every day.

About two months down the track, one of the staff approached me and said, 'You know what, when you first came, I thought you were about twelve and what the hell would you know. We all did. But you're one of the best managers I've ever had, and I don't care that you're twenty years younger than me now...I quite like it!'.

This was a lesson for me in following my gut: even when the path ahead looks daunting, if you're making changes for the right reasons and doing it by truly seeing and connecting with the people you're changing with, then stick to your guns, lay those foundations and the rest will work itself out.

Q: Particular people or influences that made a real difference to your own career supporting you in some way or believing in you?

Lead with compassion

I was so fortunate as a young therapist to be given an opportunity to work alongside some of the most well-respected leaders in my field. I was given opportunities to do things that, looking back, was a huge risk to be placed in my hands. The faith that was placed in me to 'hold my own' as I independently toured the state to train therapists and educators many more years my senior is something that I will be forever grateful for.

Kerry was my manager and mentor throughout this experience and I learned so much from her. She was someone who had a great sense of humour but an equally great sense of compassion. The way in which she spoke about people with such dignity and respect, even when they were at times being confrontational, disrespectful and outright aggressive, astounded me.

Kerry had a way of holding people to account without belittling them, challenging them to question their assumptions about others without having lived their life nor walked in their shoes. Leading others with such respect and compassion meant that respect and compassion for others seemed to follow Kerry. Walking into a room where tensions were visibly high, disengagement so apparent, Kerry would call it out for what it was, but have a way of working with people that meant that when she left the room, all of its occupants were better off for having been there.

I strive to emulate those qualities, as I know how much better an educator, therapist and person I am for having had some of the most difficult conversations with Kerry.

Believe in yourself

My mum. Well, some big shoes to fill there (size 11 actually). Mum hasn't taught me things throughout my life, she's lived the lessons to show me what life is all about. Work hard. Play hard. Keep fit. Remember to laugh. Faith is important. Know who you are. Stay true to your values. Hold your head high. Believe in yourself. Risk is vital. Failure is okay. Family is everything.

When I have felt in over my head, Mum is the one who brings me back down to Earth. It might be with a big hug, but more often than not it's by challenging me. Sounds counterintuitive to challenge someone when they're doubting themselves, but Mum does. Challenges my values by asking me is what you're doing right now something you're okay with? If not, change it up. It might be hard, but can you walk away from this knowing you did what you had to do for the right reasons?

This reminds me of who I am, what is important to me and always ensures that I lead with integrity. I know how blessed I am to have had the mum who smashed the glass ceilings and challenged the patriarchy because she has paved the way for so many more women to believe in themselves, and I am one of those women who knows how lucky and proud I am to have her as MY mum!

Q: A situation that built your resilience...

Strength in walking away

Sometimes in life and in leadership there is strength in walking away. Knowing what it is that you stand for, and will not stand for, helps to define how you will lead and who you will be happy to lead with. I was in a position where I was challenging the decision making of those around me and above me. I did not feel it aligned with our values, nor mine, and there were significant implications for a vulnerable group of people to whom I owed a duty of care. Shying away from confrontation was not going to cut it in this situation, so I had to stand up and speak out. However, the leadership in this situation didn't listen.

I continued to voice my concerns but the lack of alignment with my own values was eating me up from the inside out. It began to impact who I was at home, how I responded to my kids and my husband. I wasn't the best version of myself and it was time to walk away. Integrity is everything, and there was a strength in that moment to remind myself of who I was, what was important, and align myself with an organisation that fit with this.

What good will it do?

I have faced a situation where I have inherited significant problems from a predecessor who was much-revered. As the significant issues became more apparent, I was pressured to share this with staff and the wider community because the perception they had was not the reality of the present situation. As much as I wanted to, and could see how many problems I needed to address as a direct result of poor management by my predecessor, I asked myself and challenged those around me to ask, 'What good will it do?' It would only lead to further uncertainty for our community and jeopardise the reputation of someone who had good intent, just poor decision making.

It was a tough lesson in 'sucking it up', recalibrating with others impacted, and moving forward together.

Q: Dealing with carer responsibilities: Any insights or advice from current experience or hindsight?

This is the big one and I'm not sure anyone feels like they get this 'just right'. I was asked recently for a publication to share my 'superhero power' and while this felt awkward to say at the time, I wrote 'Working Mum'. It's a really hard juggling act. To be my best self I know I need to be fulfilled in my work life and my home life, so the following are really important to me:

- Having some non-negotiables is important. I work every second Saturday, so the Saturday I don't work I commit to going to my kids' basketball games, and my kids know and trust this.

- Mutual transparency is part of how I do things at home and work. I am open with my two young boys and partner about what I really need to do for work, when and why to help bring them into the full story more easily. Being open with your employees and employer about what is non-negotiable for you as a mum is important. I will write things into my Outlook calendar, like 'fruit duty at kinder' so that I make sure I am making my contribution when it is required.

- Photos are HUGELY important and I have photos all around my desk. This helps to remind me of who I am, and when making the tough decisions to look at the photos and ask— 'Would they be proud of their mum at this moment?' Photos also provide a 'person-first' mentality, reminding all of us that we are more than just the person we are and the people we engage with at work.

- Shoes off, trackies on when I get home (just like my mum did!). The kids know that Mum needs to take her shoes off and put her trackies on. This helps me to step out of work-mode and into mum-mode, wind down and re-connect with all my boys—the two little ones and the partner one.

Other Reflections

Lead the way you want to be led while appreciating others have a different story. You are a part of someone else's story and make sure that your input into their story makes their next chapter a better one.

LIST OF CONTRIBUTORS

Ms Nina Anderson Founder and Director, Anderson Advisory

Ms Glenys Beauchamp, PSM Secretary, Australian Department of Health

Ms Lalitha Biddulph Managing Director, Global Technology Infrastructure, J P Mogan (Singapore)

Ms Alisa Bowen Senior Vice President, General Manager Disney, Streaming Video on Demand, Disney International (USA)

Ms Abigail Bradshaw First Assistant Secretary, Enterprise Strategy Risk and Performance, Australian Department of Home Affairs

Ms Kate Carnell, AO Australian Small Business and Family Affairs Ombudsman

Ms Katie Cromie Head of Student Wellbeing and Learning Diversity, St Dominic's School, Broadmeadows

Ms Rachel Dapiran Executive Director, Strategy, Engagement and Futures, Victorian Planning Authority

Professor Jane Den Hollander, AO Vice Chancellor, Deakin University

Dr Sherene Devanesan Chief Executive Officer, Yooralla

Associate Professor Jody Evans Associate Dean of Engagement and Associate Professor of Marketing

Ms Kathryn Fagg Chair of Boral Ltd and Breast Cancer Network, Non Executive Director of Incitec Pivot and Djerriwarh Investments

Ms Christina Gillies Non-Executive Director, Consultant and Advisor

Ms Alison Hardacre Co-Founder and Managing Director, HealthKit

Professor Emeritus Andrea Hull, AO Chair/Convenor, Advisory Council of the ABC

Professor Christine Kilpatrick Chief Executive Officer, Melbourne Health

Ms Robin Kranich Executive Vice President, Chief Human Resources Officer, Gartner Inc (USA)

Ms Asa Lautenberg Director, Human Resources and Services, Samson \ Aktiengesellschaft (Germany)

Ms Lucinda Nolan Chief Executive Officer, Ovarian Cancer Research Foundation

Ms Susan Oliver Chair of Campus Living Villages and Chair of the Wheeler Centre, and Founding Chairman of Scale Investors

Ms Elizabeth Proust, AO Chairman of Nestle Australia, Chairman of the Advisory Board of the Bank of Melbourne, Board member of Lendlease Corporation

Ms Jane Sherlock Chief People Officer, John Holland

Dr Elisabet Wreme Chief Operating Officer, Guild Group and Board Member of BreastScreen Victoria and YMCA Victoria

References

Barrett, R 2017, *The Values-Driven Organisation: Cultural Health and Employee Well-Being as a Pathway to Sustainable Pathway to Sustainable Performance,* Taylor & Francis, London.

Barrett Values Centre, Mapping Values, viewed 13 March 2019 < http://www.valuescentre.com/mapping-values>

Beard, A 2012 'Life's Work: An Interview with Barbra Streisand', *Harvard Business Review,* Brighton. Viewed 13 March 2019 <https://hbr.org/2012/10/barbra-streisand>

Chambers, J 2016, *John Chambers on the Digital Era*, McKinsey and Company, New York, viewed 13 March 2019, <https://www.mckinsey.com/industries/high-tech/our-insights/ciscos-john-chambers-on-the-digital-era>

Covey, S M R 2008, *The Speed of Trust,* Simon and Schuster, London.

Ely, R, Ibarra, H, Kolb, D 2013, 'Women Rising: The Unseen Barriers', *Harvard Business Review,* Brighton, Viewed 29 March 2019 < https://hbr.org/2013/09/women-rising-the-unseen-barriers>

Gillard, J 2013, 'Julia Gillard tells of 'privilege' of being first female PM', ABC News, 27 June, accessed 13 March 2019 <https://www.abc.net.au/news/specials/rudd-returns/2013-06-26/julia-gillard-speaks-about-defeat/4783950>

Holling, C S 2001, 'Understanding the complexity of economic, ecological, and social systems, *Ecosystems*, Vol. 4, No. 5 pp. 395–405.

Leniconi, P, The Table Group 2012, *The Advantage: Why Organizational Health Trumps Everything Else in Business*, Jossey-Bass, Chichester.

Sandberg, S, Scovell, N 2011, *Lean In: Women, Work and the Will to Lead*, Knopf, New York.

Wilkinson D 2006, *The Ambiguity Advantage,* Palgrave, Gordonsville.

World Bank 2016, *World Development Report 2016: Digital Dividends*, World Bank, Washington D.C., viewed 13 March 2019, <http://www.worldbank.org/en/publication/wdr2016>

Further Reading

Ben-Shahar, T, Ridgway, A 2017, *The Joy of Leadership*, John Wiley, New York.

Crabb, A 2015, *The Wife Drought,* Penguin Random House, Sydney.

Correcha, L, Ross Walls, D 2018, *Working Mums: Stories by Real Women and How they Manage Children, Work and Life,* Finch Publishing, Lane Cove.

Isaacs, E 2018, *Winging It*, Macmillan Australia

Kelly, G 2017, *Live, Lead, Learn: My Stories of Life and Leadership,* Penguin, New York.

Nixon, C, Sinclair, A 2017, *Women Leading,* Melbourne University Press, Melbourne. MHS Assessments, Talent Products, viewed 13 March 2019 <https://www.mhs.com/Area?market=Talent#EQ2>

Sinclair, A 1998, *Doing Leadership Differently,* Melbourne University Press, Melbourne.

ACKNOWLEDGEMENTS

And some thanks

This book had a gestation over a few years. While I have written many columns on leadership over the past ten years or so, many of these were about 'professional' topics. But over the last five I have been asked to give quite a few talks and workshops that combine my professional and personal life.

At first, I found these challenging, being much more comfortable on the professional side, talking about 'stuff', rather than talking about myself and my personal journey. However, I soon became more at ease with sharing more personal lessons learned, and there certainly have been many. It is this that lead to the creation of this book.

So, first of all, thanks to my daughter, Katie Cromie, for the initial stimulus—and for sharing her own journey (so far) in the final chapter of this book.

To my Australian based Partner colleagues at NGS Global—Mark Lelliott, Kym Fletcher, Juliane Michaels, Grant Nichol, Chris Pearce and David Spencer—thanks for the constant challenge and stimulating discussions. To our broader team: Executive Officer Melinda Carbone, who provides great support, terrific organising skills and attention to details (especially in the 'not letting things fall through the cracks' area); to Jane Lelliott for working with me, questioning me and providing feedback on some very interesting engagements we have completed together; and to our clients for trusting us with the critical work that they do and being co-designers and co-learners with us.

To the female executives who shared their stories, successes, their challenges and their learnings with me and appear in this book— thank for your generosity, frankness and willingness to mentor others. And to the many other women and men who in so many ways have been the stimulus for 'putting fingers to the keyboard'.

To Lauraine Macdonald, editor and feedback giver, who helped me to 'chunk' the manuscript into 'bite-sized pieces' and generally make things more readable and accessible.

To the team at Melbourne Books, particularly David Tenenbaum for the initial encouragment and believing that the manuscript had something worthwhile to say, and to Samantha Mansell and Ellen Yan Cheng for taking the work through the editing and typesetting process.

To my partner of nearly fifty years, Robert, who is a superb diplomat, great listener, who knows when to ask how things are going, offer some advice (or a coffee or red wine) and when to just keep out of the way. The best advice I can ever give anyone is to choose your life-partner very carefully. There is likely no more important decision you can make. Thank you for being my partner and my best friend.

To our children, who have always considered their mother quite normal (I think!), even if she does some different things at times. They have encouraged me to keep on doing what I'm doing—even if only because when I come to a sudden stop, I might want to start organising their lives and they'd rather I didn't have that extra time.

And to the grandchildren, particularly those into, or emerging out of their teens, with whom we have very interesting conversations about where their passions and dreams might take them. May there be something useful in this work for you.

ABOUT THE AUTHOR

For the past twelve years, Marianne has been Managing Partner and co-owner of NGS Global, an international leadership advisory business. Prior to that she was a Group Vice-President and then Senior Vice-President of the US headquartered professional services firm, Gartner Inc (listed on the NYSE). She has held a Chair of Management, and been Associate Dean and Professor at Melbourne Business School, University of Melbourne, and led that School's Senior Executive MBA. She is now a Distinguished Academic Fellow of MBS and a Fellow of the Australian Institute of Company Directors. She was a Finalist in the Telstra Business Women of the Year and is a mentor for women and men, as well as for organisations. She has been a regular judge for *The Australian* Innovation Awards, and co-founded the Australian chapter of international engaged-philanthropy group, Social Venture Partners. On the personal side, Marianne and her partner Robert have four adult children and a bunch of interesting grandchildren.